Flash Cartoon Animation

Learn From The Pros

Glenn Kirkpatrick
Kevin Peaty

friendsof

DESIGNER TO DESIGNER™

an Apress® company

Flash Cartoon Animation

Learn From The Pros

© 2002 friends of ED

ISBN-13 (pbk): 978-1-59059-207-6
ISBN-10 (pbk): 1-59059-207-7

Printed and bound in the United States of America 9 8 7 6 5 4

Distributed to the book trade in the United States by Springer-Verlag New York, Inc., 233 Spring Street, 6th Floor, New York, NY 10013 and outside the United States by Springer-Verlag GmbH & Co. KG, Tiergartenstr. 17, 69112 Heidelberg, Germany.

In the United States: phone 1-800-SPRINGER, e-mail orders@springer-ny.com, or visit http://www.springer-ny.com. Outside the United States: fax +49 6221 345229, e-mail orders@springer.de, or visit http://www.springer.de.

For information on translations, please contact Apress directly at 2560 Ninth Street, Suite 219, Berkeley, CA 94710. Phone 510-549-5930, fax 510-549-5939, e-mail info@apress.com, or visit http://www.apress.com.

The source code for this book is freely available to readers at http://www.friendsofed.com in the Downloads section.

Credits

Reviewers
Toni Laukka:
www.apukeittio.com
Mata Haggis:
www.matazone.co.uk
Tim Jones:
www.animaxinteractive.com

Editorial Board
Steve Anglin
Dan Appleman
Ewan Buckingham
Gary Cornell
Tony Davis
Jason Gilmore
Jonathan Hassell
Chris Mills
Dominic Shakeshaft
Jim Sumser

Managing Editor
Sonia Mullineux

Commissioning Editor
Andy Corsham

Editors
Jon Bounds
Libby Hayward

Project Manager
Vicky Idiens

Graphic Editor
Ty Bhogal

Proofreader
Cathy Succamore

Indexer
Simon Collins

Cover Design
Kurt Krames
Katy Freer

GLENN KIRKPATRICK

Born angry in 1964 it doesn't take Glenn Kirkpatrick long to realize there are serious problems with the world. Despising society for its relentless pursuit of banality and compromise he embarks upon a lifelong campaign of visual terror that eventually leads to this book.

1982: Cuts his teeth on television animation during the Saturday morning animation wars of the late 1900's while working for companies such as Hanna-Barbera and Walt Disney in Australia and Japan.

1990: Is recruited by major American production companies into a special operations unit of animation directors for missions deep into the heart of Asia. While under his command as layout and animation supervisor, over 150 half hours of television animation are produced for children and adults alike including high profile series such as "Rugrats" and "King of the Hill".

1999: Returns to Australia having been groomed for a top slot in the corporation. He goes for himself instead.

2000: Learns Flash and creates the first Spawn of Satan cartoons. Tries to get them played on the Internet, his attempts are restricted. Seems people didn't dig what he had to tell them.

2001: Stages operation www.funnyazhell.com with combined local forces Kevin Peaty; it's rated a major success.

2002: Forms Australia's premier flash animation studio, Funnyazhell Animation, which currently produces high quality Flash animation for the web and broadcast television.

Someday this war's going to end...

KEVIN PEATY

Kevin has been involved in the animation industry for twenty five years, working for companies such as Hanna-Barbera and Walt Disney. In that time he has worked as a character animator, animation character lead, animation director and unit director on projects for television, direct to video and feature films.

He's worked on films he's proud to have been involved in and some he'd rather forget... but that which does not kill you makes you stronger and rather than become bitter and twisted, or as well as becoming bitter and twisted, he chose to turn his formidable talent and skills to the world of net animation. His long time friend and colleague Glenn Kirkpatrick convinced him that as well as giving almost total freedom to air his vile and misguided views, the Flash program would guarantee Peaty unparalleled fame and wealth. Kirkpatrick, using the forum of his subversive and morally suspect web site www.funnyazhell.com, introduced Peaty to a dark, subterranean world populated by disenfranchised 2D animators every bit as sick and pathetic as they were.

And the rest, as they say, is history.

Peaty continues to work in the animation industry as well as produce Flash films of dubious intent. He lives with his wife Lianne, his son James and two cats in Coogee, Australia where the local Montagnard tribepeople worship him, like a God.

3: ART DIRECTION   49

4: STORYBOARDING   69

10: OUTPUT & PUBLISHING   245

OVER TO YOU   263

INDEX   265

INTRODUCTION

It was the best of times, it was the worst of times. New technology had created amazing opportunities for the animation industry to realize ideas never before thought possible. The impact of this technology has meant that studios have had to restructure and adapt to a changing marketplace. The demands of an increasingly sophisticated and discerning audience and the response of studios trying to keep pace with those demands has meant that the artists involved in the business have had to learn and adapt, or fall by the wayside. Studios have come and gone. Some markets have dried up while others have appeared.

Computer animation has taken over from traditional 2D animation as the medium of choice.
The more things change, the more they stay the same. Animation is still created by animators, a good story is still a good story, a great film is a great piece of entertainment and a computer is really just another pencil, albeit a very sharp one!

From its humble beginnings a century ago, animation has grown into a business generating millions of dollars a year. Major film studios invest enormous amounts of money and employ the talents of hundreds of artists and thousands of executives on a single animated film, usually resulting in impressive box office returns.

From scratchy black and white silent shorts, through to the introduction of color and sound, animation has embraced the latest technology to produce films of amazing virtuosity and scope. TV, feature films, 3D; animation has expanded into many and varied arenas.

This genre of filmmaking came to be defined by large budgets, crews, and numbers of executives, and the opportunity for the lone artist to present his singular vision seemed largely lost - if in fact it ever existed. The constraints of big budgets and bigger investors tends to take the edge off any artistic statement.

Where was the platform for the maverick animator, unencumbered by investors, focus groups, marketing gurus and money? Ironically the answer came from the aforementioned new technology: The answer was Flash!

Flash animation and this book

Flash was a program designed for web designers and then co-opted by a few canny traditional 2D animators who realized its potential immediately. The limitations of this simple program only fuelled greater ingenuity and creativity. In Flash one artist can do it all....for next to nothing!

Making animated films in Flash can be a liberating experience, whether you're a jaded 2D animator looking for an opportunity to express your pent up angst, or a complete novice to animation and filmmaking who is looking for the opportunity to unleash your artistic statement on an unsuspecting public. Flash allows you opportunity with little or no money or artistic compromise.

Flash also offers the chance to display your film on the Internet, accessing a huge and varied audience.

In this book, we will show you how to make a film. We will take you through the entire process, from initial idea to finished work. We'll examine the process step by step.

If you don't know how to animate, we'll show you that as well; first the principles of animation and then how to apply these skills specifically to Flash. It's our intention to give you a better understanding of the principles of animation and filmmaking and how we have found they can be adapted to this program.

We will take you on a guided tour of the animation production process, with detailed explanations of each step, from beginning to end. By the end of this book, you will have the filmmaking, animation and Flash skills to confidently tackle any idea and translate it into your own personal visual statement.

There are many books on the market that can show you how to use the Flash program. Very few actually address the potential of Flash as an animation and filmmaking tool. We want to utilize the flexibility and simplicity of Flash as a platform, allowing the individual to explore his or her potential as a filmmaker.

We both have a lot of experience working as animators, character leads and animation directors for the major animation studios in the traditional 2D field. When we discovered Flash, we were immediately drawn to it. It empowers the individual and allows you total autonomy, unique in the film industry.

This book will take you through the filmmaking process sequentially. We'll show you how to make a Flash animated film using a case study, 'The Boy Who Cried Wolf', so that you can see how the principles of animation and filmmaking work in the real world.

We'll build 'The Boy Who Cried Wolf' the same way any animated film would be built, so the process is clear to follow and easily adaptable to your own project. Let's look at the production process from beginning to end:

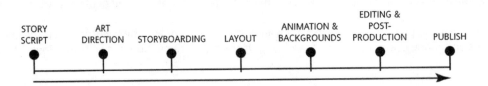

This is the order in which a Flash film is made and is the one we'll be following in this book.

Whether you're a web designer who wants to expand your knowledge of animation and to further exploit the potential of the Flash program, a would-be animated filmmaker who lacks the knowledge or experience to take your ideas further, or a Flash user with some skills but no idea how to employ them, then this book is for you.

Follow the lessons and examples laid out in this book and we can guarantee you that you'll be able to make animated Flash films that look professional and that rise above the majority of films made in this way at present. All you have to do is come up with the ideas!

From the editors - using this book

We're as proud of this title as Glenn and Kevin rightly are, and hope you enjoy reading it - as well as learning a lot from two very well respected animators. Before you rush off and enjoy learning to animate, please read this section as it will help you get the most from the book.

Download files

There a wealth of graphics, Flash FLAs, and sound support files available for this book. They aren't essential to use this book to the full, as everything in the book can be built from scratch - your way. But, if you'd like to see exactly what the authors have done, or build your version of their film, then they are organized by chapter at www.friendsofED.com.

Layout conventions

We want this book to be as clear and easy to use as possible, so we've introduced a number of layout styles that we've used throughout.

- We'll use different styles to emphasize things that appear on the screen, KEYSTROKES OR SHORTCUTS and also web addresses.

- If we introduce a new **important term** then these will be in bold.

> *If there's something you shouldn't miss, it will be highlighted it like this! When you see the bubble, pay attention!*

- When we want you to click on a menu, and then through subsequent sub-menus we will indicate to like so: File > Import... . This would translate to:

File	Edit	View	Insert	Modify	Text	Control	Window	Help

New	Ctrl+N
New From Template...	
Open...	Ctrl+O
Open as Library...	Ctrl+Shift+O
Close	Ctrl+W
Save	Ctrl+S
Save As...	Ctrl+Shift+S
Save As Template...	
Revert	
Import...	Ctrl+R
Import to Library...	
Export Movie...	Ctrl+Alt+Shift+S
Export Image...	
Publish Settings...	Ctrl+Shift+F12
Publish Preview	▶
Publish	Shift+F12
Page Setup...	
Print Preview	
Print...	Ctrl+P
Send...	
1 the boy who cried wolf.fla	
2 the boy who cried wolf.fla	

- If there's something you should type in then it'll be 'in single quotes'.

1. If there's a practical exercise for you to follow then the steps that you have to follow will be numbered.

2. Follow them through, checking the screenshots and diagrams for more hints.

   Further explanation of the steps may appear indented like so.

3. When you get to the end, you can stop.

friends of ED forums and feedback

All books from friends of ED aim to be easy to follow and error-free. However, if you do run into any problems you can visit our community support forums at www.friendsofed.com/forums for advice, ideas, solutions, and inspiration. Maybe you have a problem with a certain file or tutorial, or you're just plain confused about a particular topic - leave a message on the forum, and your fellow Flash designers and animators will get you sorted in no time! And be sure to sign up for our monthly newsletter at www.friendsofed.com.

We'd love to hear from you - even if it's just to request future books, ask about friends of ED, or tell us how much you loved this book, e-mail us at feedback@friendsofed.com.

> *Visit* www.friendsofed.com *to get the latest on books, free sample chapters and tutorials, community gossip, and links to some of the slickest sites online today!*

1: STORYLINE & SCRIPTING

The first step on the road to making your film is to have an idea. Fortunately, coming up with an idea for a film is easy – you can adapt almost anything for a film script. Unfortunately, coming up with a good idea that can be developed into an entertaining film is slightly less easy. This chapter will help you to refine your basic idea, structuring it into a number of scenes and a version that should prove easy to storyboard and develop.

There's nothing as valuable as an original idea, or as rare. If you think you've got one, then don't squander it. Scribble your thoughts down as soon as you can, and let your imagination run. Make every effort to turn it into a film that will at least be equal to your initial concept.

On the other hand, don't get bogged down by the hunt for that elusive original idea. Originality is highly prized, but it has never been a prerequisite for an entertaining film. Hollywood especially, has never been over burdened with original thought!

When thinking about what you want to say in your film, bear in mind the context: you're new to this. You should be thinking about making a short, fairly simple, but outrageously entertaining Flash film. So keep the concept simple. You want your ideas to be related to the audience in an easy, direct way.

Our considered advice is not to attempt anything too taxing until you have become more comfortable as a Flash animator and filmmaker. Later on, of, course you can tackle that dense, profound dissertation on man's inhumanity to man that's been in the back of your mind for years. But for now, keep it simple!

> *A simple concept allows you more freedom to polish your film and make it more visually entertaining.*

In this chapter, we'll look at how to take a story, write it down as an outline or treatment, and then turn that into a script. However, before any of this, we've got to come up with an idea, so here we've got a few pointers as to what you may need to think around.

Idea

The idea, or concept, that you devise to base your film on is entirely up to you. There's no list of story ideas for beginners, though as you're reading this book, you've more than likely got at least one.

If you are searching for an idea, then the best thing to say is don't - one will come to you eventually, someone will tell you an anecdote or a joke, or you'll remember an incident from your own life.

Whatever the idea will be, you can't force it. Books, films, TV, music are all great places to start thinking of what kind of story can work well - watch a lot of videos!

If you're really stuck, you can always turn to a traditional story or fable and add your own twist, it's certainly never done Walt Disney any harm!

For the purpose of demonstrating the process of making an animated film in Flash, we've decided on a story that everybody knows. Apart from the familiarity of this story making it easier to be used as a learning tool, it also allows us to condense and generally take huge liberties with the narrative. We can assume the audience knows the story of 'The Boy Who Cried Wolf'. Having said that, the story should be able to be understood by someone who is not familiar with it. We hope to demonstrate how such a clichéd idea can be relatively funny and entertaining.

Things to think about

Whatever you're thinking of, a couple of very important points to keep in mind are:

What kind of film are you trying to make?

Scary, funny, dramatic, whatever - watch as many films in that genre as possible (as well as plenty outside it), digest everything, it'll seep into your creativity without you knowing it. With the animated format you may want (or have) to take a lot of shortcuts, but watching great films animated or otherwise will give you the best idea of what can be done.

Who is your audience?

The subject matter and content of your film should be addressed with your target audience in mind. How you relate the story will depend on who you anticipate your target audience to be. If you have the Internet in mind as the forum for your work, then you can be a little more liberal in your approach.

You may be thinking of entering your film into a film festival, in which case you may have to compromise, or at least modify, your language or subject matter, but that's totally up to you. The authors of this book would never advise or condone such a course of action. If you want to compromise, join an animation studio!

Will they find it funny?

Humor's a funny thing. What people find funny is incredibly subjective. The French, as a nation, find Jerry Lewis funny - we certainly don't. The lesson is; don't aim your humor at the French.
Unless, of course, you are French, or you find Jerry Lewis funny.

Is your audience going to like slapstick, or are they Woody Allen fans? If your film is going to be based on a joke, then try and make sure it's funny!

Will they find it boring or pretentious?

There is no sin worse than boring the audience. Confuse them, irritate, offend or upset them, but don't bore them! Being pretentious can really get an audience offside. Without a receptive audience, all your hard work can be for nothing.

> *Alienate your audience by all means - just make sure do it for the right reasons!*

Be critical

As with every other area of the filmmaking process, be self-critical. Write down your idea and reread it as many times as you can. Don't start patting yourself on the back just yet. One of the greatest things about Flash is that it has given the individual filmmaker a voice. We don't have to pander to corporate sensibilities or the bland, lowest common denominator. If ever there was a stage for eccentric film making, Flash is it. Eccentric is one thing, bad is another. You want to reach the audience and get your message across. Making the weirdest film in the world requires some structure.

Watch your film, or read your script, looking for what's wrong with it - what seems weak. It may be a negative way of thinking, but if you don't do it, others will. There'll be plenty of time to bask in the glory later on.

Story

Within the confines of a short animated film, you'll have less room to get a complex, non-linear (for example, 'Pulp Fiction') narrative across. But, as with anything creative, there are no hard and fast rules: get your idea down on paper and you can refine it as you go along.

The best bet is to keep your story within the confines of the classic three-act structure, with a beginning, middle and an end. These elements don't necessarily have to come in that order, but they should all be there.

Beginning

This is where you set the scene and introduce your main character. You need to grab the audience's attention and then draw them in. Ideally, there should be a key to the motivation of your main character that will lead to the later action. For instance, in our story, the boy is bored and looking for fun.

Middle

The bulk of the action will take place here - this is where the tension is built-up via a series of events that will lead ultimately to the climax. If you were going for a longer film, you would develop your characters and plot here, but for most animated shorts the story itself is more important than in-depth character analysis.

End

The conclusion should contain the payback to the previous two scenes. If you're making a comedy, you need a good, strong punch line here. If you've built up a scary ghost story, you need either a chilling end or a satisfying, "And all along it was the janitor" Scooby Doo style finale. Our tale finishes with the moral to the story. A strong ending will ensure that people want to come back to look at more of your work, a fizzled-out finish will make your film instantly forgettable.

Tone

You may be forgiven for thinking that Flash animations work best with upbeat jokes and light stories. This is partly true, but there are many fine exceptions to this rule.

Check out the work at Whitehouse Animation Inc (www.whitehouseanimationinc.com), where you'll find 'Kunstbar', which demonstrates a fantastic amount of different drawing styles, as well as being well animated:

At the same web site (specifically at www.whitehouseanimationinc.com/cub.htm) you'll find 'Cub' by Steve Whitehouse which is in our opinion the best Flash film of all time.

Are you sitting comfortably?

It's now time to look at our story:

The Boy Who Cried Wolf

Once upon a time there was a young shepherd boy, who had to keep watch over his sheep day after day to make sure that they came to no harm. One day, he was sat watching his sheep, and he was very bored. For a joke, he decided to yell out, "WOLF! WOLF!".

The villagers came running to help the boy. But there was no wolf and the villagers were very angry. "Don't cry wolf if there's no wolf!" they said.
He grinned naughtily.

The next day, the boy was minding the sheep and again, he was bored. Once again he decided to yell out, "WOLF! WOLF!".

Again, the villagers came running. Again, there was no wolf. And lo, they were so angry. They cried, "Why WON'T you stop yelling wolf? There's no wolf!".

The following day, the boy was tending his flock, and suddenly he saw a big, bad, scary wolf. He was very frightened, and he started to scream, "WOLF! WOLF! WOLF!!!"

But the villagers thought he was joking again and nobody came to his assistance. When the boy eventually turned up in the village, he was very upset. The wolf had killed his sheep.

A villager said to the boy, "We thought you were kidding, nobody believes a liar, even when he's telling the truth".

THE END

This is the abridged version, but you get the general idea. Now what we have to do is get the essence of the story and adapt it so that we can build a script.

Outline

We now need to start thinking in terms of what we can communicate visually rather than literally. In feature films, screenplays are often adapted from novels. This requires knowing what can be translated to the screen, what will work visually, and what information can be communicated visually without the audience explicitly being told.

Whatever you think, it always takes longer than you would think to reproduce something from the printed page on the screen. Think just how much has to be left out when translating a novel. The answer, which forever taxes screenwriters, is to reduce it knowing what can be left out while still retaining the integrity of the original work. Outlining the plot will also give you a firm idea of exactly what the major characters do, and who they are.

The pitch

Most stories have a moral, or a pitch (a couple of sentences, or even a few words – used to sell the idea), which communicates the essence of the tale. This is extremely helpful in knowing exactly what you need to tell the story, what is less important, and what can be cut out.

Let's look at our story and condense it, keeping just the basics of what it's about:

```
If you lie, then you won't be believed even when you're telling the truth.
```

...knowing this can be a boon when attempting to crystallize the story further into a sequence of actions or important happenings that push the story forward.

The story of 'The Boy Who Cried Wolf' boils down to these main points:

```
A bored boy, minding his sheep.
He yells "Wolf".
Villagers react.
He yells "Wolf" again.
Villagers react again. Not as enthusiastically.
He yells "Wolf" again...this time for real.
No-one reacts.
Disaster!
```

Now we have the basis for a script, describing in words what we can build as a film, scene by scene.

Script

The script is where we break down the film into scenes. A scene isn't to be confused with a camera shot – it can contain any number of these. A scene is one section of the story, usually confined by location and time – although those again, are rules that can be broken.

For the first time, we have to think visually. Like a play, a film script has to contain all the information that will finally be communicated, both visually and verbally. It would generally contain any special costume or make-up requirements, any vital information about the setting of the scene (place, lighting, time, whatever), and any specific camera movements that are essential for the story to be told.

An animated feature often contains more specific shot information at script stage than a live action film. This is due to the extra work involved in building each shot. For example, a live action director could easily film shots of our 'Boy' from a number of different angles, whereas each shot for an animator requires a great deal of extra work. The earlier camera decisions are made in the creation of an animated film, the less unnecessary work will need to be undertaken. Try to imagine the film in your head and write down how the camera will relate it to the audience.

It can help in the process of working out scenes if you think of the state of affairs at the start, and at the end of each of your actions. You can then work out exactly what has to happen, and what has to be communicated to the audience to get from one state to the other. In our film, this is a little over-simplified maybe, but the more involved that your cartoons become, the more the work put in at this stage will bear fruit.

The shots and scenes have to supply the audience with a wealth of information, they'll need to understand the motivation of the characters, the physics and natural law of the film's universe – and as an animator all of these things are under your direct control.

The Boy Who Cried Wolf

This is the script that we've worked up for our film; we've included as many camera directions as we can decide upon at this stage:

Scene 1
```
FADE IN.
WIDE SHOT. EXTERIOR DAY.
SHEEP ON A HILL GRAZING. SUNNY, BUCOLIC SETTING.
TITLE (OVER SHOT).
"THE BOY WHO CRIED WOLF"
TITLE FADES OFF.
CAMERA PANS ACROSS PAST SHEEP TO A TREE.
BOY SITTING UNDER THE TREE.
VILLAGE IN THE DISTANCE.
CAMERA PUSHES IN ON BOY.
```

This opening scene is an establishing shot, showing the audience where the story is taking place, panning across the landscape, then trucking in on the boy, leading the audience to where they are supposed to be looking. This pan and truck in set-up is a standard opening shot much used in TV animation.

Scene 2
```
CLOSE ON BOY.
ALARMED. HE YELLS "WOLF!".
```

Scene 3
```
VILLAGERS REACT PANICKED.
YELLING AND SCREAMING!
WIDE SHOT, ZOOM, PAN?
```

This shot may be a wide shot, it may involve panning or zooming. We can solve this problem in the storyboard phase.

Scene 4
        MEDIUM SHOT OF BOY.
        SMUG. "JUST KIDDING".

We don't want as tight (close) a shot as Scene 2, as this shot is not as intense.

Scene 5
        VILLAGERS. MEDIUM SHOT.
        CONFUSED. "HUH?".
        FADE TO BLACK.

Fading to black implies the passing of time.

Scene 6
        CLOSER ON BOY.
        "WOLF!!".

Slightly tighter than Scene 2 this will help build the drama.

Scene 7
        VILLAGERS.
        SCEPTICAL. "REALLY?".

Slightly wider than Scene 3, as we want this shot to be less intense.

Scene 8
        BOY SAME AS SC.4.).
        STILL SMUG. "NO!".

Scene 9
        CLOSE UP ON BOY.
        SCREAMING. "WOLF!!!".

Tighter again than Scene 6, building the drama.

Scene 10
        VILLAGERS.
        ANGRY NOW. "SHUT UP!!".

Maybe tighter on the villagers as they are angry. We want this shot to be more intense than previously. We can address this problem when we draw up the storyboard.

Scene 11
        EXTREME CLOSE UP ON THE BOY RUNNING, PANICKED.
        "OH NO!!!!".
        PULL OUT TO REVEAL WOLF CHASING BOY.

Scene 12

```
HEADSTONE.
"R.I.P. THE BOY WHO CRIED WOLF".
THE END.
```

We've taken huge liberties with the original story. We've also left out a lot of detail. The fact that this story is so well known allows us greater latitude when paring the story down.

We've killed the boy off at the end of our film. Why? It was quicker and easier to script it that way. We also thought it was funnier (in a black kind of way). The idea of a village elder lecturing the boy about truth and lies sounds incredibly dull and long-winded. Don't bore the audience, or yourself! It still has the same basic message and hopefully will be conveyed to the audience as such.

Refining the script

In traditional animation studios, the board artist pitches his board to the director to see if it's working in the way the director imagined. The board artist will pin his storyboard panels onto a wall and talk the director through the sequence.

Very rarely is the desired storyboard delivered at in one pass. We'll say this more than once throughout this book: a film is something you build. When we adapt this script to the storyboard, we, have a better idea how it plays. We can fine-tune the film as we go.

Warning - don't skip the script!

To get your film to this stage, you may not need to go into quite the detail we have here. You've got an idea for a Flash film, so you feel you can go straight to the storyboard. This is possible and probably the way a lot of Flash animators work, especially early on when the films are quite simple – but it can cause problems.

Human nature being what it is and us creative types being kind of impulsive and undisciplined, most filmmakers will take what they think is a great idea and run with it. Then, halfway through, they realize they don't have an ending - or the ending they do have stinks. In major feature films, one of the recurring problems is a story with no ending and these are highly trained (or at least highly paid) professionals!

If you've written a script from your original idea and feel that it can be translated into an entertaining film, then you can approach the storyboard with a lot more confidence than someone who thinks he can make it up as he goes along. The storyboard should also be much easier and quicker to build.

It's better to follow all of these stages. As you become more proficient as an animator and filmmaker the more ambitious your films will become. When this happens, you'll ignore these early steps at your own peril. One day you could wake up and find you've wasted six months on a completely indecipherable film...with no ending! It happens to better filmmakers than us.

Over to you

What you need to do now:

- Think of an idea for your cartoon, making sure it's suitable for your audience. For inspiration, look to traditional fairy stories, urban myths, jokes, films and campfire ghost stories.

- Write a basic version of the story to get the plot written out. Has the story got a beginning, middle and end? If you're making a funny film, are you sure it has a good punch line?

- Outline the film as a series of actions that will be the basis for each of your scenes. At this stage, you may find that your story is too complicated, so prepare to do some editing or think of creative ways to simplify it.

- Use this outline to write a script, adding as much detail about the finished film as you can at this stage. As well as thinking about dialogue, start to think about camera directions and special effects.

By now you should be developing a strong idea of how your film will work, in the next chapter we'll look at how you can use Flash as a sophisticated drawing tool to start realizing your ideas.

2: DRAWING WITH FLASH

Flash provides a platform for the animator to achieve just about anything that's possible in traditional 2D animation and a few things the traditional animator could only dream of. The drawing tools available in Flash, whilst not strictly designed for the character animator, prove remarkably adaptable to that task. You should by now have decided on what story your film is going to tell, this chapter will give you the skills to draw your characters and backgrounds in Flash.

What animators have learned is that there is always untapped potential lying within this simple yet remarkably flexible program. Using these tools to achieve the required results takes ingenuity and cunning. Luckily, they have been mined for their animation potential and we present them here. These are not the only uses these tools can be put to in the quest for more and different animation. As you become more comfortable within the Flash environment, you'll no doubt discover new ways to combine and adapt the tools in this program to produce unique and remarkable results.

Take these tools and the functions discussed here as a starting point, you will develop in your understanding of them as you use Flash – open it up now and try each one out as we discuss it. As your own style of drawing and animation evolves, there may be some tools that you use more than others, or you may end up working in a totally different way to us – it really is up to you.

> *If you already have some experience of drawing within the Flash interface, then parts of this chapter may not be new to you, and you should feel free to skip them – it may be as well to read it all to remind yourself though.*

Tablets

It's important to mention that in order to get the best out of these tools, you will need to get a drawing tablet. This is a piece of hardware you connect to your computer that will act as your pencil and paper. There are several different brands available and they come in a range of sizes. The choice is yours. We use an 6" x 8" tablet as it's big enough to draw on, yet not too cumbersome or expensive!

It is possible to draw in Flash using your mouse, but after you get a drawing tablet you'll wonder how you ever did.

The Tools panel

Let's look at the tools available in Flash. Most of the tools for drawing in Flash are available by simply selecting them from the Tools panel, which should be visible as soon as you open the program. The main ones we will be concerned with for drawing are:

The letters in brackets are keyboard shortcuts to select each tool; E for the Eraser tool for example.

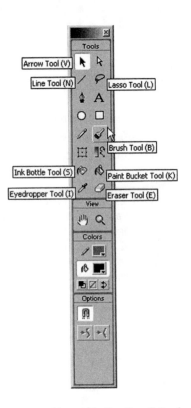

Brush tool

Most beginners to Flash make the mistake of overlooking this tool and start working with the Pencil tool instead. Because the name implies that it can be used as a pencil, it seems like a good place to start. While it can be used to draw, the line is thin and unappealing compared to the brush, especially if you're using a pressure–sensitive drawing tablet.

After you select a tool you'll notice that the Options box at the bottom of the toolbar will change and a variety of different settings will become available for the tool you've selected. With the Brush tool it will be the following:

As this tool will be the one we will be using most, it's good to experiment with all the different settings to find the ones you like, we can only cover the settings that we use a lot in detail.
Set the Brush Mode to Paint Normal.

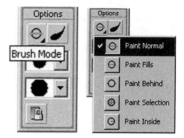

The next icon along is the Pressure tab.

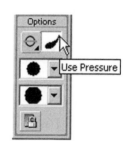

This is a great feature when used with a drawing tablet to achieve a nice brush line. You'll find that as you press harder or more softly on the tablet with the pencil, the thickness of the line will vary.

Line without pressure sensitivity   *Line with pressure sensitivity*

Try making thin lines, thick lines, curves, thin to thick and vice versa. Experimentation is really the key here. If you concentrate too much on the tool you're using it's going to mess up your work! It's only a tool and it should be as easy and as invisible to use as normal pencil.

The other settings are;

The Brush size setting – this will determine the width of your line. Select the appropriate brush size for the drawing you're doing;

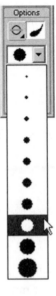

The Brush Shape setting acts as a kind of calligraphy tool. We'll set this to round.

Line color with the Brush tool

As Flash treats the brush as a paint tool rather then a drawing tool the line color when using the brush is linked to the Fill Color. To change the color of your line you must therefore select the Fill Color in the color section of your Tools panel to change the color of the brush.

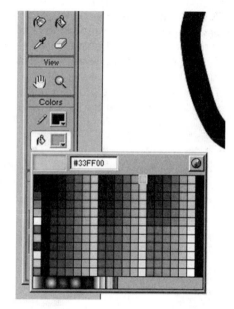

Paint Bucket tool

This tool is used for filling shapes with color. We will use this tool to color all our drawings. Since the Brush tool is linked to this tool for color we can also use it to change the color of our lines even after we have finished our drawings.

There are not many settings for this tool but those we have can save us a lot of time if properly understood.

The main option available to us for this tool is the gap size setting. This will determine the way the tool fills shapes. If you have a drawing where the lines are not completely joined and this will happen a lot when doing your animation especially when optimizing curves (more on that later), then the tool will need to be set depending on the size of the gap in the line. If Flash detects a gap in the line, then it will not fill the area with color unless you adjust the setting.

You can see in this example the circle on the right has a break in the line, therefore when you try to fill this area with the gap size set to "Don't Close Gaps" it wont work. If you adjust the gap size to "Close Large Gaps" Flash will treat the line as if it were unbroken and fill the circle. There are limits to how large the gap can be of course and some times you will need to adjust your linework, closing the gaps.

The more you use the program the more familiar you will become with which setting to use and know instinctively what you can fill and where you need to join up your lines.

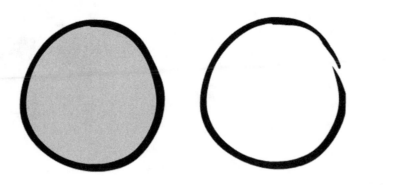

If you just adjust your gap setting to Close Large Gaps, then Flash may not be able to fill smaller areas in your drawing, this is especially noticeable on sharp corners of shapes

Until you become more familiar with this tool, try Close Small Gaps first. Flash will then fill most areas with color whether the line has small gaps or whether the drawing involves smaller areas to be filled.

Eraser tool

The Eraser tool works in much the same way as the brush except it erases rather that paints. The options for this tool are similar to those of the Brush tool also. We always set them the same, as otherwise it's very easy to get confused. We've set our mode to Erase Normal.

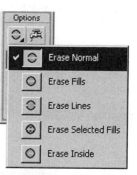

The shape setting works the same as for the Brush tool, set it to suit the drawing your doing.

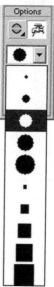

The Faucet setting, when selected, erases entire color fills or entire sections of line. It can be toggled on or off by simply clicking on it. Try it out on one of your drawings, it

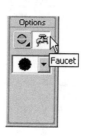

Although the Eraser tool is very handy, the most useful and constantly used function in drawing with Flash is the undo function.

Using undo as your Eraser

This will remove from your drawing the line, fill or whatever you did last. It works not only on your drawings but also on every operation you perform in the program.

> *You can use the undo function by selecting* Edit >Undo, *however it's best to get into the habit of using the keyboard shortcut for this operation which is* CTRL/⌘ + Z.

You'll find as you become more adept at drawing in Flash you'll have one hand on your mouse or pencil and the other poised above the CTRL/⌘ + Z buttons.

There is also so a redo function that works in exactly the same way except it will redo whatever you just undid, Edit > Redo or CTRL/⌘ + Y.

Line tool

Unlike the brush, which Flash treats as a paint tool, the Line tool is a drawing tool - more like the pencil. We do most of our drawing with the brush, this is not to say that there is anything wrong with using the Line or Pencil tools and in some situations it can prove better to use them. You can achieve a level of precision that is very difficult to achieve with the brush.

The main difference between the two is the look. These drawings were done with the Line tool and the Brush tool, respectively.

Line tool   *Brush tool*

You can clearly see the difference between the two, they are both nice drawings in their own way and which style of line you prefer will inevitably be up to you and the type of film you are making.

The Line tool is however much more difficult to use especially when trying to draw images for animation. It operates in an entirely different way to the brush in that you don't draw with it like you do with a pencil. To use the Line tool you draw lines by clicking a certain part of the stage then moving to another part then releasing the mouse button thus creating a straight line between the two points. You must then draw another line connected to the last one and so on. Then adjust the lines with the Arrow tool until your desired drawing is created.

The advantage the Line tool does have is that drawings created with it are always smaller in file size. Also, any drawing requiring a lot of straight lines that won't be needed to animate, for example props such as furniture or a car, are sometimes best drawn with this tool.

It is possible to create 'brush-like' pictures using the Line tool, but not without a little effort. We feel it's best to start with a rough drawing done using the brush, then clean it up using the Line tool.

Using the Line Tool

1. Draw or import your 'brushed' version. If you'd like to use ours, open `LineToolPractice.fla`, which can be downloaded from www.friendsofED.com.

2. Select the all of the brushed version and change its color to a light gray so you can see your darker line stokes easily. CTRL/⌘ + A will select all of your drawing, and you can use the Fill Color drop-down in the Property inspector.

3. In order to make sure that all your lines are connected to each other you will need to turn on your snap to function. Go to Edit > Snap to Objects this will also ensure the areas within the drawing can be easily filled.

4. With the Line tool selected choose a line width with the Property inspector at the bottom of your screen (it's known as Stroke height in Flash).

You can also set your color and the type of line (Stroke style, in Flash - dashed, hairline, and more) here.

5. We've used a Solid Stroke with a height of 2 and black color.

6. You will need to create a new layer above the rough drawing for the Line tool drawing. Click on the Insert Layer icon, bottom left on your timeline.

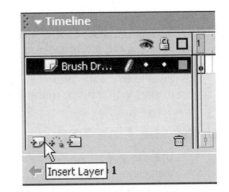

7. Rename it 'Line Drawing', click into its name and simply type in your new name.

8. Lock the brush-drawn layer, with the dot underneath the padlock. This will prevent you altering it as we go along.

Now on this layer we're going to draw lines from all the main points on your rough drawing.

9. Select the Line tool and click at a corner of your brushed picture, and drag your pointer over to the end of that particular curve.

10. Repeat this for all of the curves in your drawing, for our example we're only drawing round this young chap's hair.

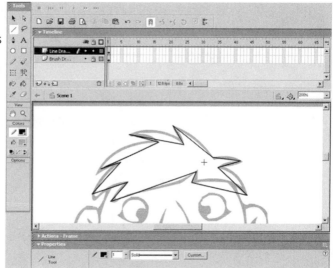

As you'll learn many times in this book, animation is easier if you can separate, and hence separately animate, different parts of your characters. This is a technique known as **limited animation**, but more, much more, of that later.

11. Next select your Arrow tool, touch it on the middle of a line watch how the pointer gains a curved line around its bottom:

12. Then click and drag to bend the line into the shape of the drawing below. You will need to do this for all of the lines you've drawn.

13. Some of the lines may curve twice, to split a line - first bend to follow the first curve:

14. Then ALT-click at the apex of the first curve - notice that a circle appears around the head of your pointer

15. Drag the circle along your curve to the point where it becomes a second curve.

16. Then tidy up your two separate curves as before.

17. You can continue to refine your lines, bending them in the center to better match your drawing or moving the corner points.

Notice how the line beneath your pointer becomes a right angle, when you move the Arrow tool pointer near to the end of a line.

It's best to use this drawing method in conjunction with the shape tools such as the rectangle and circle as well as the pencil. In the example above, the head and eyes could be drawn using the circle tool. This simplifies what can be quite a difficult process.

As you can see this can be a tedious and time consuming way to draw but it does have its uses.

Removing overlap

When drawing this way you can overlap lines then delete parts of the line by highlighting it with the Arrow tool then pressing DELETE/CLEAR, this feature is not available with the Brush tool where everything of the same color gets joined into one puddle.

Here's an example with a circle and a square:

Color with line tools

All line tools are treated by Flash as drawing tools so changing colors with them is linked to the stroke color and should be adjusted here.

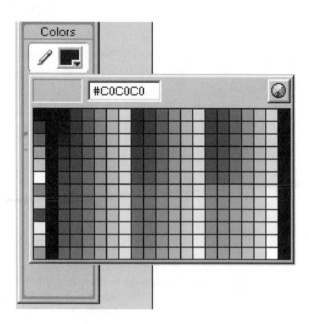

The Ink Bottle tool colors the Line, Pencil and Shape tools in the same way the Paint Bucket tool colors the brush. You can change any colors of your line with this in the same way.

Adjusting line width

You can also adjust the width of your line after you have finished a drawing with this tool by selecting a different line setting in your Property inspector at the bottom your screen.

One of the most useful functions of this tool is thickening up lines drawn with the brush.

You can see here that this is the same drawing just with a thicker outline, a style that has become very popular in animation these days.

To achieve this look select the Ink Bottle tool, select a line width then touch the outside line of your drawing and the Ink Bottle will add a line to the outer edge of the drawing.

This is a separate ink line and not part of the brush line, so any color changes you make to this line will need to be done with the Ink Bottle not the Paint Bucket tool.

> *If you're going to use this approach its important to make sure you save all your drawings as symbols, especially if you intend to reuse them at different sizes otherwise you will notice problems with the fill line becoming to thick or thin.*

Eyedropper tool

This tool is used to reselect color or lines from images that you have already created and can save you a lot of time when coloring your drawings. It works with all the main brush and line tools and is linked to both the Fill Color and the Stroke Color.

When the Eyedropper tool is selected, whichever Color selection box is active will be set to the color of anything you click on. In effect you can pick up any color - for use with your drawing tools.

You will have many drawings of the same character and you will need to color them all the same. This tool enables you to select one drawing, pick any color from that drawing, then simply fill the next drawing without having to look at your color palette.

Arrow tool

All the tools we've just discussed are basically your pencils, pens and paints in Flash. The arrow tool although not exactly a drawing or painting tool is the one that you will undoubtedly end up using the most. It is what we use to select objects on the stage to move them and to edit them. It is also the tool we will be using to do all our work in the timeline and to select all the other functions in Flash.

> *To switch quickly to the Arrow tool while using another tool press the CTRL/⌘ key, this will toggle to the arrow key as long as the CTRL/⌘ key is held down , when released it will switch back to what ever tool was selected, with practice you'll find this a really time saving trick.*

Selecting objects

There are basically two types of objects in Flash, those that have been created as or converted to symbols, and those that have not. Which type of object they are will determine how our tools, and in particular the Arrow tool will affect them when you select them on the stage.

Symbols

Any object that has been converted to a symbol will not be able to be immediately edited on the stage. Therefore when you click on it with the Arrow tool a blue line will appear around the entire image. If you hold down on the image you will be able to move it around with the mouse or by using the arrow keys on your keyboard.

This drawing has been converted to a symbol and when selected with the Arrow tool the blue line appears around the image. It can now easily be moved anywhere on the stage.

Non symbol images

When you select images that have not been converted to symbols you'll notice something entirely different will happen.

In this example of the same image that has not been converted to a symbol, when selected with the Arrow tool only the part of the image selected will be highlighted, in this case the hair which includes the entire outline of the character:

If we now try to move this image selected like this Flash will move only the part of the image that was selected. The features and colored part of the jumper stay where they are.

In order to select the entire image you will need to select it in the timeline, or to drag a square with the Arrow tool around the entire image - do this by click-dragging from one corner of an enclosing rectangle to another.

Letting go of the mouse button with leave the entire image selected. While it is selected, you can now move it around the same as with a symbol.

> By holding down the SHIFT key with an area selected, then selecting another area with the Arrow tool you can select additional parts of the drawing to move or edit.

Lasso tool

The Lasso tool, like the Arrow tool is used for selecting images or, more importantly, parts of images and is very useful when making your drawings.

For example, say we have just finished our drawing, and we decide that we want to change the position of the arm to make it slightly lower, instead of having to redo the entire drawing, we can simply select the arm by drawing a line around it with the Lasso tool then move it independently from the rest of the drawing.

Select the Lasso tool, you can then select individual areas by clicking and drawing a line around them.

Flash will highlight exactly which areas are selected, be sure to check that you've drawn around the parts you wanted.

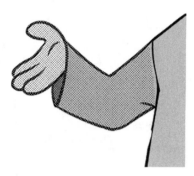

With the arm selected we remove it from our drawing and place it into the clipboard by Edit > Cut or CTRL/⌘ + X.

Create a new layer for it below the existing layer in the timeline and paste it in place there by hitting CTRL/⌘ + SHIFT + V.

You can now move it the to a new position. Then copy the body layer and paste it on top of the arm in the new layer, delete the old body layer and you have your new modified drawing.

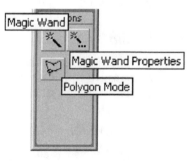

This technique takes a bit of practice but will save you a lot of time once you get used to it.

Lasso tool options

The Options section of the Tools panel has three buttons that can be used to alter the way in which the Lasso tool works. The Magic Wand option allows you to individually select color areas, where as Polygon Mode changes the way that the outline of the Lasso is drawn. With Polygon mode selected, you can draw a polygon around the area to be selected, Flash draws the outline of the selection as a series of straight lines joining consecutive mouse clicks.

There are a few other tools in the Tools panel, those we just covered are the main ones related to drawing in Flash, and the ones we will most use. Some of the other tools will be covered later in this chapter as we start to use them to produce our animation.

Symbols

Symbols are without a doubt the most important element in creating animation in Flash. All our images in the film will eventually become symbols and most of these symbols will become our **key poses** (key points in the animation) as we'll discus in depth in the Animation Principals chapter.

So what exactly is a symbol? In most Flash books you read a symbol is described as an image that Flash stores in the library that can be reused over and over again without needing to be reloaded, thus reducing the size the final movie.

Apart from the fact that they reduce the file size and bandwidth of our movie, for us as animators (rather than web designers), they are more importantly the basis for all the action that will take place in our film. For its only after a drawing has been converted to a symbol that it can be motion tweened to create movement, which is what animation is really all about.

There are basically three different types of symbols in Flash, graphic symbols, movie clip symbols and button symbols. Let's look at the differences between these types of symbols:

Graphic symbols

The graphic symbol for animation (unlike web design) is the most important type of symbol we will use. A graphic symbol is an image that Flash stores in its library that we can re-use when and where ever we need. More importantly, it is the type of symbol that we can use to create movement with the use of motion tweening.

Graphic symbols do not have to be a single, static, image we can also create and group any number of images into a graphic symbol to use as a cycle or a particular movement. Some people may argue that its best to use a movie clip symbol for this function and maybe they are right in some situations. The main problem with movie clip symbols is that you can't watch them as easily in the timeline when making your animation so for our purposes we'll be doing all our animation as graphic symbols.

Movie clip symbols

The movie clip symbol is basically a type of symbol used to create a movie within a movie, and used mainly for interactive type Flash projects. That's not to say that you can't use it making Flash "films", but for character animation graphic symbols are more suitable.

Button symbols

The button symbol is also an interactive element in Flash. It is important to point out that for most films made for the Internet you might want to attach a button at either the beginning of the movie to start to play it once its loaded or at the end of the movie to replay it once it's ended or both. We'll cover this briefly when we look at publishing your movie in our final chapter.

Converting an image to a symbol

Let's take a closer look at exactly what Flash does with these images.

In this example we see a character that has been divided into body parts that have been placed on separate layers. The arm layer is selected in the timeline and the contents of that layer are highlighted on the stage.

To convert the image to a symbol, select Insert > Convert to Symbol or F8.

Then label it, in this case 'sc01 arm', set it to a graphic symbol, and click OK.

Flash has now converted our drawing to a symbol and placed it in the Library.

35

The Library

When we convert an image into a symbol, Flash stores the symbol in the Library so that we can access it easily to use later in the film. Let's now take a look at the Library and see exactly what it is and how it works.

To open the Library in Flash, select Window >Library.

You should now be able to see a new window with a list of all the symbols we've created so far in alphabetical order. In this case, there is one for each part of the character: his arm, body, eyes and mouth.

If you select any item in the Library, you will be able to see a preview of it.

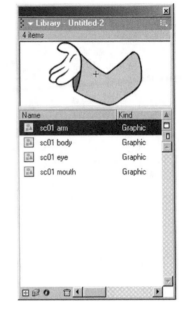

Organizing your Library

It is essential when animating in Flash to clearly label all your symbols. It's best to start labeling them with names that you will easily be able to recognize and it's also sometimes a good idea to include the scene number from which the symbol is used in order to keep things in your library organized.

There are, of course, many different ways to organize your Library, and you are bound to find a method, which will eventually become a personal choice. In our example, we have organized our Library according to the elements within each scene. This is to provide you with a look at how to go about doing this, don't worry about following our system to the letter. The more drawings you make, the more you will need to consider how you name and organize things. Being aware of this at the beginning will however save you a lot of time, and how you eventually organize your Library will ultimately be up to you.

Something we find very useful is to create new folders in your Library for each scene or character that you can place all your symbols in. All this will really help you find exactly what you're looking for in your Library as you start to create more and more symbols.

To create a new folder in your Library, click on the small tab in the right top corner of the window, then select New Folder.

Flash will now have placed a folder in the Library. To name this folder, double-click on the default name and type in a new name – we've called it 'scene 01'.

To move your symbols into the folder select them, (you can select more than one by holding down the SHIFT key), then drag them into the folder.

You should now have a folder for scene 01 with all your symbols for that scene placed in it.

This is important because you could end up with hundreds of symbols by the end of your film.

Placing symbols on the stage from the Library

To place a symbol from the Library into a scene, first select a layer in the timeline where you want the symbol, then select the frame you want the symbol on. Select it in the Library, then while holding down on it, drag it onto the stage. It should now appear on the stage and in the timeline on the frame you selected.

Editing symbols

As we've discussed, you can't edit a symbol on the stage the same way you can with an image that has not been converted to a symbol. In order to edit a symbol (in other words make changes to the drawing that has been converted to a symbol), you must edit the symbol in the Library. It's important to note that any changes you make to a symbol in the library will mean that every Instance (everywhere you have used the symbol in the movie) of the symbol will also be changed.

To edit a symbol, first select it in the Library, then select the tab at the top right of the symbol window and click Edit. Alternatively, you could simply double-click on the symbol to edit it.

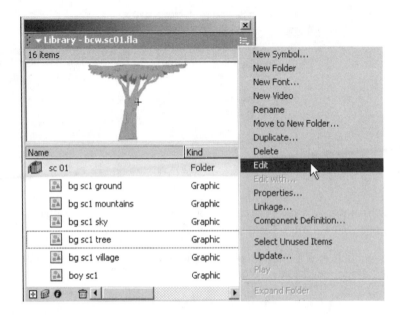

What will happen next is that Flash will open up what appears to be a new scene. This is the timeline for the symbol and the new stage is where you can make any adjustments to the symbol.

Another way to edit symbols is to click them on the stage with the right mouse button (CTRL-click on the Mac) this will open up a context menu from which you can select Edit Symbol.

From this same menu, you can also chose the Edit In Place. This option allows you to edit the symbol in place on the stage.

Below we have chosen to edit the symbol of the man's body. Flash has opened up a new timeline for the symbol and we can now make any changes to the drawing that we want.

Remember whatever changes you make here will affect every instance of the symbol in the movie.

If you look just below the far left-hand side of the timeline, you'll notice that next to Scene 1 (the scene we were in when we went to Edit Symbols mode) is the name of the symbol we're editing, in this case sc01 body. To exit Edit Symbols mode and return to the scene click on Scene 1 .

You'll notice that the instance of the symbol on the stage should now contain any changes you made.

Each symbol has its own timeline. It's possible to create a symbol that contains more than one drawing and also more than one level. We'll discuss this in more detail later in this chapter and later in the book when we start to create cycles.

Breaking apart symbols

We've just learned how to edit symbols. Now suppose we have a symbol that we've used in a previous scene and we want to use the symbol again in a new scene, however this time we want to change the symbol slightly, but not have the changes effect the previous instance of the symbol.

We have our character gesturing with one hand, his body symbol has his left hand drawn together with the entire body, but in our new scene we want him to gesture with both his hands,. Instead of having to redraw the entire symbol of his body, we can break apart the existing symbol on the stage, make our changes and save it as a new symbol so as not to effect the previous instance of it.

To demonstrate:

In this example, we have created a new scene (Scene 2) and we have copied and pasted all the symbols and layers from sc01 here. Next we want to select the symbol of his body either in the timeline or on the stage so that the blue square around it is visible.

To break the symbol apart (convert it back to a normal drawing) select Modify > Break Apart or CTRL/⌘+ B (it's really helpful to learn and get used to using the hot keys for functions like this as it will save you a lot of time when animating)

Flash should now have converted the symbol back to a normal drawing on the stage and it should be highlighted. You can now make your changes to the drawing. Once done, select the drawing in the timeline then convert the new body image to a symbol for this new scene. The original symbol (sc01 body) will still be in the Library unchanged.

Another way of doing this is to use the duplicate symbol function that is covered later in the chapter.

Symbols within symbols

Since each symbol has its own timeline, it's possible to have more then one drawing in a symbol. This can be either as a series of different levels to make up a single image or as a series of images over time, for example, a cycle (we'll discuss this further in the cycles section of the chapter).

We can also place symbols within symbols. We've cut to our character in Scene 2 and we want him to stand mindlessly in the same spot for the entire scene. In order to save layers, we can combine all the symbols that make him up and create a single symbol that will be the entire image.

There are several ways to do this, but since we want him to remain in exactly the same place in this scene, we will copy him and paste him into one new level.

First select all the levels, then copy them, Edit > Copy or CTRL/⌘ + C. Next create a new layer and paste them onto that layer, Edit > Paste in Place or CTRL/⌘ + SHIFT + V. After you've done this you can delete all the other layers, leaving only the new layer.

You can see that Flash has placed all the symbols together in the one layer. With this new frame selected in the timeline, you can convert it to a symbol just as we did with the separate drawings.

Flash has combined all the symbols that make up the man and grouped them together as a new symbol.

If you look at the symbol in Edit Symbols mode, you'll see that Flash has done exactly the same thing in the symbol timeline as it did in the scene; combined all the symbols into the one layer.

Sometimes we will want to have more than one layer in the symbol timeline, especially when we start to create cycles. In order to create the same symbol, but with each element on a separate layer, we will need to do things a little differently.

First select all the layers in the scene as we did before but instead of copying them with Edit > Copy, copy them with Edit > Copy Frames or CTRL/⌘ + SHIFT + C this will copy them exactly as they are in the scene on separate levels. Next select Insert > New Symbol (CTRL/⌘ + F8).

Name your symbol and click OK, this will open up a new timeline for the symbol. Select the first frame in the layer and paste the frames there. Edit > Paste Frames or CTRL/⌘ + ALT + V – this should have placed all the layers into the symbol timeline, and created a new symbol in the Library

To place this new symbol on the stage, go back to Scene 2 and create a new layer on top of the others. Select the symbol in the Library and drag it into position over the existing image.

You may have to move it around a bit to get it exactly in place. Once you have, delete all the other layers.

You now have the same symbol only with all the separate layers in the symbol timeline. This type of symbol will really come into play when we start to create cycles.

Optimizing drawings

We've talked briefly about the effects of optimizing lines in the Art Direction chapter and we've covered the basics of using the Brush tool to draw our images at the beginning of this chapter. Let's take a closer look now at how we optimize our lines to give our drawings that nice cartoony look.

When you optimize an image in Flash (particularly when it was drawn with the Brush tool) the program is basically reducing the amount of lines and curves in the image. Each brush stroke is not an exact straight line. With the Brush tool, each line is seen by Flash as a shape, not a line, and therefore a single straight line from the brush tool may include several individual lines.

This simple triangle drawn with the Brush tool would appear to be three lines, but as you can see, it actually contains a lot more lines and curves tha you would think. After optimizing the shape, it appears almost identical, but you can see that the actual image size (in computer memory terms) has been reduced by 75%.

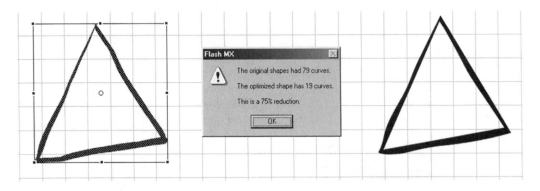

You might not be able to reduce more complex images quite as much, but you will still notice a very substantial reduction.

So apart from giving our drawings a smoother, more polished look, optimizing lines effectively reduces the size of our images and in turn our entire movie.

Optimizing lines

In this example we have a drawing that was done with the Brush tool. We've deliberately drawn this image a little rough to get a better contrast between what the image will look like after it has been optimized.

There are a few different options available for optimizing your lines but the one we will use the most will be the Optimize setting.

Select the drawing you wish to optimize in the timeline, then select Modify > Optimize or Ctrl/⌘ + Alt + Shift + C.

A new window will appear with a slide setting in it labeled smoothing. This control will determine the degree to which Flash will optimize the lines in the drawing.

When set to None, the amount of smoothing will be very minimal, and when set to Maximum it will increase.

Optimized at just above none

Optimized at maximum

As you can see by the above examples the amount of smoothing you apply to the drawing can dramatically affect the final look. The eyes, for example, have been affected quite differently.

Repeating this process more than once will also increase the degree Flash optimizes the drawing.

There are no set rules about how much smoothing to apply to a drawing to get a certain look, it's something that will always require a few tries to get what you want. You'll often find that after you've optimized your lines, you'll need to go back in with the Brush tool and the Eraser to make a few small touch-ups to get the drawing looking exactly as you want it. It's really a matter of trial and error. The more you do it, the more instinctive it will become.

Some tips for optimizing lines

Resizing the stage before you optimize your lines will change the effect the optimizing function has on the look of the final drawing. For example, here is a drawing optimized at maximum, but in the first example, the stage has been scaled up to 400%, and in the second, it has been reduced to 25%.

Optimized at maximum with the stage at 400%　　*Optimized at maximum with the stage at 25%*

Top tips for optimizing images

- When optimizing images you can select certain parts of the image and optimize them separately.

- By using the Arrow tool to select only the body, we can optimize it without the eyes, nose and mouth. You can then select these elements to optimize separately where you may require more or less smoothing.

- Selecting parts of the image with the Lasso tool will have the same effect and allows you to be even more intricate with parts of the image you want to optimize.

- In this case, the body only was optimized.

Straightening curves

Another method of optimizing your line is the **Straighten Lines** option. This is more effective when you want to optimize images that are made up of straight lines, like buildings in backgrounds or props, like furniture etc.

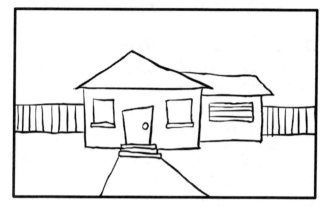

This example of a simple house, drawn with the Brush tool, looks very rough and crude, but after we optimize it with the straighten function, it takes on a whole new look.

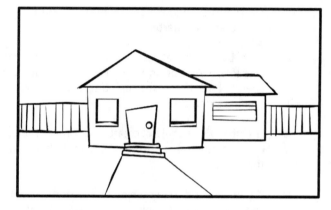

To straighten lines, select the image in the timeline then select Modify >Straighten

When straightening lines, there is no way to adjust the amount of straightening. It's sometimes necessary to make small adjustments to the lines before and after applying this option. Getting used to using the undo shortcuts (CTRL/⌘ + Z will help speed up the process.

Smoothing lines

There is also a smooth lines option – Modify > Smooth. This can be used more for images drawn with the Line tool as opposed to the brush.

Optimizing line work and drawings in Flash is the easiest and most effective way to give your artwork a professional look. The Optimizing tool immediately gives your drawings a classic, toony appearance, as well as reducing file size. No wonder Flash animators have embraced this tool with such gusto!

The degree to which you optimize your pictures is up to you as the animator. Try it and see. With the undo function (the animator's best friend!), experimentation is easy and fun. Push it to the limit and then bring it back a notch.

It's important to try and give your film a unique look, so see how optimizing your artwork affects the look of your drawings and whether or not it suits the style of film you're after.

Develop your own style

The drawing and painting tools in Flash are exactly that – tools. By following along with our experiments here you should have a better understanding of how the process of drawing characters and backgrounds works, but there's a lot more to making animated films than that.

Right from the start you'll have to make difficult decisions about what the whole look and feel of your cartoon will be, and next up we're going to give you as much advice from our own experiences as we can in this respect. At the end of the day, though, it will be your choice.

Over to you

Now you need to experiment with Flash until you feel comfortable with the interface and tools. Here are some ideas to get you started:

- Start by making a basic cartoon character made out of simple shapes, this character won't be in your final film, so don't worry about realism or style. Spend some time experimenting with different lines and colors, remember there are no rules.

- Use the Brush tool to create your images, and remember to place separate elements such as arms and legs on separate layers so that you can animate them later.

- If you have a drawing tablet, use as often as you can. It may take a while, but soon you'll wonder how you ever coped with just a mouse. If you don't have a tablet – think about investing in one!

- Practice using the Line tool to clean up your images, leaving them bold and clear.

- Finally, make some rough drafts in Flash of some of the characters in your film – again don't worry about perfecting them now – they will develop as your project progresses.

In the next chapter we'll start to think about style and artistic effects. For now, just enjoy making Flash your new sketchpad.

3: ART DIRECTION

*Once you have decided upon a good storyline to use for your film, it is then time to consider the style of your film and its visual appeal. In this chapter, we'll consider the importance of making good artistic decisions from using color to convey mood, to creating characters that are easy to animate. We'll also look at how to create **Model Sheets, Size Comparisons** and **Backgrounds,** and throughout, we will focus on maintaining clarity with good line work. Let your imagination run wild and then think of practical ways to realize your ideas.*

The visual elements that comprise the look of your film will influence how the audience reacts to what they see and how they are involved in the story. As well as dialogue, action, music and staging, art direction will convey the mood and tone of your film. What we have to consider here is how the tone of the story is reflected visually and how the mood of certain parts or specific sequences is conveyed. For instance, to convey a somber mood, we may use subdued colors and to impart a sense of danger, we could make heavy use of sinister shadows.

Now is the time to ask a few important questions:

- What visual style are we after?
- How do we make a visually cohesive statement, marrying background and character elements so they look like they occupy the same universe?
- How do we present our film considering our limits as animator?

Art direction dictates the overall look of a film. This really is a part of the process when you can let your imagination soar. Look at your favorite films and take what you can from them. Don't feel limited by the genre. The strength of Japanese animation (at least the best of it) is that they don't seem to feel constrained by the fact they're making animated films. They have more in common with Ridley Scott than Walt Disney.

'The Iron Giant' is one American animated feature that doesn't seem constrained by the medium. It stands as a wonderful film in its own right, rather than being just a great animated movie. Refer to live action films for ideas as well as the work of guys like Chuck Jones and Brad Bird ('The Iron Giant', 'The Simpsons').

How do we make the film we want to using Flash? Well, we have to tailor our story to fit the limitations of the Flash program. We also have to be constantly mindful of file size and how the film will stream on the Internet. This doesn't mean we have to forget about the more ambitious ideas. What it does mean is that we have to use ingenuity and cunning! With some thought and careful planning you can fake some pretty impressive shots, camera moves and effects in Flash that can still stream smoothly.

> *Art direction, particularly color styling and background design, is one area where we can make a Flash film look as good as films created using other formats, as any choices made here should have little effect on file size.*

What design elements do we use to achieve this cohesive visual statement? For our purposes, we can divide them into line work, color/tone and design. We should create our characters and backgrounds with these elements in mind.

Line work

Unlike live action films, **line** is an integral part of the overall visual style. Cartoons were originally preliminary drawings used by artists when painting pictures or frescoes. These were line drawings only, with no color and little or no shading. In classic animated cartoons such as 'Bugs Bunny' and 'The Flintstones', the line work to a large extent, defined the look of these shows, not only in the character design, but the backgrounds as well.

Since 'Ren and Stimpy', with its unashamedly retro look, line work has made a comeback as a dominant design element. With many animated cartoons seeking to emulate the success (both artistically and commercially) of 'Ren and Stimpy', this retro, line-heavy, style has dominated animation for the last decade or so. Animated shows displaying this strong visual style offer us a vivid example of how art direction can elevate what are sometimes quite average cartoons to a more entertaining level. When this kind of art direction is combined with good stories and memorable characters such as the John Kricfalusi-directed 'Ren and Stimpy', then animated classics result. 'Space Madness' is as close to a perfect animated film as you can get.

Black line

Consider the following examples of the same character, rendered with different line work:

Here the character is drawn with an even, unobtrusive black line. The line has little impact on the overall look of the drawing. This is not necessarily a bad thing. Maybe you don't want the line work to make a bold visual statement. The line doesn't have to be dominant.

In this example, the line work is much *toonier*. It varies in thickness and has much more vitality than the first. It also makes a much stronger visual statement and is a more significant element in the overall look and art direction. This type of thick/thin line work has always been popular in animation, particularly Saturday morning TV. It is the type of line historically favored by comic book artists and cartoonists.

Another example of line work as a significant design element. Here we have the outside line rendered a lot heavier than the interior line work. This approach has made a comeback in animation over the last few years.

These examples would most likely be rendered as a black line.

Self-color line

The alternative to using a black line, which resembles the old Xeroxed line when animation was copied onto cel before being painted, is to color style the line work so that it complements the color of the character's skin, hair, clothes and so on. For example, the line used on the skin area could be color styled a darker pink than the actual skin color.

In this drawing, you'll notice the line used to describe the sweater is actually lighter than the fill color. Obviously, you can't go darker than black, so a lighter color is required to show the interior line work. Daffy Duck is a good example of lighter color styled line, though his outside line remained black. Often, **self-color line work** is used in conjunction with black line.

Color

Color can influence how the audience feels or interprets what is happening onscreen. More obvious examples of how color can convey mood are a blue palette to represent coldness or night. A red/orange palette shows warmth or heat.

Color can also represent danger, good, evil or any number of moods or ideas. What color is good or evil? Pretty much whatever color you decide, as long as it is consistent. The scenes in a Wicked Witch's house could be color styled yellow and pink, as long as evil is consistently represented by this palette. The audience is subliminally told that these colors represent evil or good. This is another factor supporting the point you're trying to make, the story you're trying to tell. Color alone won't tell your story, but combined with all the other factors will help lead the audience in the right direction, making your point easier to communicate.

The colors you choose are a personal choice. As with most areas of filmmaking, there are no hard and fast rules. Make sure your character's colors work with the background colors. They have to look like they exist in the same world and at the same time be able to be differentiated by the audience. We don't want the character "lost" in the background. For example, a character positioned against a blue sky in a sky blue shirt may appear as a head floating in space. If we color style his skin tone to be sky blue as well, he'll pretty much disappear!

An individual's perception of "what works" is highly subjective, so experiment with color choices and never underestimate their importance.

Design

The look of the characters, backgrounds and props you draw and render is entirely up to you. What you think looks appropriate, reflects the story you're telling or is just a style you think looks good is an individual choice. When getting started, simplicity is probably best. Don't over extend yourself and learn to be critical of your own work, especially when making films in Flash as you'll more than likely be working alone. Learn to step back and look at your film as much and as often as you can at every stage of production. Frequently, the temptation is to plough ahead. It can become quite tedious watching the same footage over and over again, but this process will reveal any problems and/or shortcomings in the film.

The overall design is about making a cohesive visual statement, one that is sympathetic with the story and ties the disparate visual elements together. Look at films you like, live action as well as animation, for ideas and inspiration.

Characters

The story you're trying to tell will, in most cases, be largely told by the characters. What they say, what they do and what they look like will tell the audience what kind of characters they are, how the story relates to them and the dynamics of their relationships with each other. What they look like, how they act and the things they do depends on them having a defined personality. This personality should be reflected in your character design or at least be a significant consideration. Sometimes it can be more effective to design a character against type. For example, the bad guy doesn't always have to be big and threatening or a Snidely Whiplash type. These are creative choices that are up to the individual, but they must be considered and now's the time to do it, not as you're animating your film. Otherwise you can end up with a cast of characters that have little in common and don't look like they inhabit the same universe.

Character design, how you draw them, and the style you employ will be largely influenced by your own personal taste and style, as well as your own drafting ability.

Keep it simple

Don't make the job more difficult by designing characters that are going to be difficult to draw or move around. You will probably end up having to draw your characters in many different positions and angles as well as be able to animate them from pose to pose. If the design lends itself to these tasks, the job is a lot less ponderous and animating more fun. You're more likely to try different ways to illustrate the story and be a little more adventurous.

This character, apart from looking like the product of someone's bad dream, would be a nightmare to move.

Walking, especially would be particularly time consuming. Acting, gesturing, even blinking (!) could be problematic. Think long and hard about introducing twelve legged creatures and then only if they sit-out the entire film.

> *Keep the design simple. Your animation will only look as good as the drawings you do.*

Costume design can add something to your film. This could be a nervous breakdown. Be careful of patterns and complicated or intricate designs.

The feather would also have to be animated whenever the character moved. That's not to say don't use costume elements like feathers, just be mindful of the added workload.

But not too simple

Take a look at our stick man:

This approach is perhaps too simple. You could have great difficulty entertaining an audience with stick figures. The fact that it has already been done (and to great effect) notwithstanding! If you choose to use stick men, you better have an exceptionally strong story...

Characters that are drawn too simply make it harder for the animator to convey emotion. Although easier to draw, this kind of design makes acting difficult.

Separate elements

It's often best to design your characters so that they're able to be broken down into separate elements. This is a technique which really came into its own with the advent of television animation. Known as limited animation (as opposed to full animation where the entire character is drawn in every new movement), it can save much drawing time, while, if used thoughtfully, can be very effective. More recent manifestations of this genre have driven it into disrepute. This has more to do with cost cutting and bad animation than the inherent shortcomings of the style.

Earlier examples of limited animation, as pioneered by studios such as Hanna-Barbera, were strong on visual style and entertaining to watch. This was due to good stories, good characters, strong art direction and animation, even though limited, done by experienced animators. Quite often television shows made in this way were far more entertaining than more expensive feature animated films. The greatest examples were often the most limited...Rocky and Bullwinkle and Roger Ramjet come to mind. If these shows were made now, they would more than likely be made using Flash. These separate elements can be heads, arms, legs, eyes, mouths etc., depending on what's required of the character.

When designing your characters, keep the idea of separate elements in mind. In this example, we've allowed for the separating of eyes and mouth. We've given these elements enough room to do what they do without impacting on the rest of the face.

Separating the eyes allows you to make the character blink without having to redraw the whole head.

Separating mouths allows you to animate the character's dialogue without redrawing his whole head (or his whole body!). More of this as we start to draw and animate our characters in Flash.

We can separate elements of the whole body in exactly the same way.

If we have a scene where we want the character to gesture, then we can separate his arm.

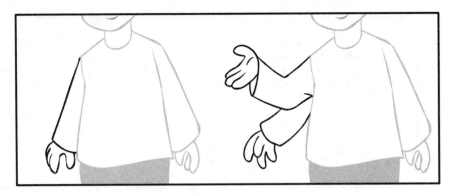

Separating the legs allows you to animate **walk** or **run cycles** without redrawing the whole character in every frame. (See the Animation chapter).

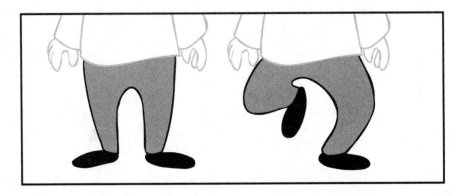

Consider the importance of your line work. One of the most pleasing aspects of the Flash program is the way it handles line work; how it can optimize and straighten the line to give a very *toony* look. This is something seized upon by 2D animators when first finding their way around the program. It's also one way of telling who has animation experience and who doesn't. Flash animators with little or no experience sometimes fail to grasp the significance of this important tool.

In these two drawings of the same character, the second conveys a much stronger visual style. It feels more dynamic and alive. The line work in the first version seems weaker and less decisive. Apart from being visually less pleasing, it may have an impact on the way the audience reacts to the character and the story in general. Maybe they will be less involved in the narrative or even being distracted from it. When we want them to be focused on the story; they may be thinking "...what a crappy drawing!" (based on personal preference only....the authors views are his own and etc.etc.....!)

Model sheets

When drawing and animating a character, consistency of **model** is essential. From key drawing to key drawing the character has to look the same, even when being stretched or squashed. This is especially important when the character is being handled by a crew of animators. Individual artists have their own individual styles. So, there needs to be enough reference material for animators to be fairly sure they're all drawing the same character.

This is the difference between drawing on-model and off-model, with or without reference to a **model sheet**. The main element of any character reference is the model sheet. These usually comprise a turnaround (the character in a pose, seen from different angles: front-on, profile, rear-view, front three quarter and rear three quarter), different attitudes on the head, different poses and some key drawings pulled from scenes that have really nailed the character. With all this reference material, do animators all draw on-model? Well, no! But guaranteed, they're closer than they would be otherwise.

Our model pack doesn't need to be anywhere near as detailed as that required by a team of willful, recalcitrant animators - as we're going to draw all the animation ourselves in Flash. It is, however, useful to have some reference.

The cast

Always start with a rough drawing when drawing any character: whether it's for the model pack, layout or in the actual animation process. Learn to construct your characters from basic shapes, and then add the detail. Like the film making process, drawings are something you build. Working rough when exploring character ideas allows you a lot more freedom and a looser approach to design problems. Once you're happy with the result, then you can clean it up.

> *In animation studios, the clean-up stage is not handled by the animation team, but a completely separate department, but in our case we are animator and clean-up technician all rolled into one!*

As these drawings are for model reference only, we can leave them in the rough stage.

Spinning them around

Once the character has been designed, we need a **turnaround**; seeing the character from several different angles.

Take your first drawing (the front on view) and use that as a reference for the other drawings. It's important to maintain consistency of proportions and the relationship of the features to each other.

Boy

The main character in 'The Boy Who Cried Wolf', the Boy, will need a basic turnaround. We can solve any design problems that arise when seeing him from different angles and will give us the freedom to animate him from most angles without having to think to hard about it.

The other characters aren't as prominent as the boy. We only need one drawing of each to give us the required reference - this is a decision that, if made early on, can save a whole host of effort in your work. Let's introduce the supporting cast of The Boy Who Cried Wolf.

The Sheep

One sheep model is enough. You've seen one sheep; you've seen them all! The sheep in this film will probably not need to be animated at all as we only pan past them in the opening shot. We can just draw them in slightly different poses, or in a different color - and of course, in Flash we can edit different instances easily.

The Villagers

We can get away with one female and one male. We can reuse them, animating them slightly differently and placing them in different places on the stage. Making them bigger or smaller, depending on whether they are in the foreground or background. If needed, we can also vary the color styling to make them look different.

The Wolf

We only see him in profile. So one profile drawing will suffice.

Character size

In a normal model pack in a studio situation, where more than one animator is working on the film, we would also put together a **Size Comparison sheet** (or **Size Comp**). This is a line-up of all the characters to show how they measure up against each other. It helps the animators and layout artists not only draw the characters the right size in relation to each other but to get the right eye direction in one shot when a character is looking at another off-screen character.

Size Comps also give you an early indication of how the characters look with each other, whether their heads are the right size. Do they look like they're the same species (if they're supposed to be)?

This is what a Size Comp should look like. We don't need one for all our characters as we can adjust them in the film as we go.

If later on you work on something more ambitious, with a larger crew, then size comps are invaluable.

Backgrounds

Backgrounds are the environment, the universe in which the story takes place. The look of any film relies on the way the characters and props fit into and interact with their environment. Well-designed backgrounds and interesting (and appropriate) camera moves can forward a story without any animation whatsoever. Backgrounds can be interesting, even impressive, without distracting from the acting or action. There needs to be empathy between what the characters are doing, where the story is going, and the backgrounds in which these are unfolding.

How you approach each background depends on where you want to use it and what kind of shot it's going to be.

Establishing shots

These are primarily about the background, since they are showing the audience the environment and the location of the characters. Any characters are shown in the context of the background.

In closer shots, the background is a backdrop to the action, or acting, taking place. Care must be taken not to detract from the character animation with too much detail, or a palette that is too heavy or unsympathetic.

> *It's important that the characters are not lost in the background, but stand out so the audience can clearly follow the action. Be careful using the same colors on the background as on the characters as this can create confusion.*

Generally, the tighter the shot, the simpler the background should be. In this close-up, we've kept the background very simple and uncluttered so as not to distract the audience from the acting.

You'll notice in this setup, the background is out of focus to create a greater sense of depth. Soft focus effects such as this cannot be done in the Flash program, but must be imported into Flash from another program such as Photoshop.

This depth of focus effect looks great, but remember that imported backgrounds of this type can increase your file size quite markedly, so must be used judiciously when making films for the Internet where file size is important.

In addition to this, be careful when using bitmap backgrounds in Flash, as camera moves can also be affected. For instance, a slow truck-in on a vectored character and a bitmap background could look jittery, if the bitmap starts to look pixelated as we zoom into it, since vectors can be re-drawn at a sub-pixel level and bitmaps (by definition) cannot. Registration issues can become more complicated. There are also various techniques for preparing and importing Photoshop backgroundss (or other elements) into Flash.

Backgrounds used in close-up shots can be sometimes as simple as a **color card**. A color card is a flat color that matches the color of the area of the key background, with absolutely no detail. These don't distract from your characters acting.

Color cards were used to great effect in 'Ren and Stimpy'; not only as normal backgrounds, but as tools to convey different moods and emotions. Color cards have also been used in traditional 2D animation to imply an explosion; exposing different colored cards for a frame at a time over a short period of time...say 8 to 24 frames. Usually primary colors: red, yellow and blue.

When designing your backgrounds, it is best to start with the establishing shots or long shots of each location. Once you've got these done all the other backgrounds of the same location can be drawn to match them. In many cases you can reuse the main background key by repositioning or enlarging it to suit the other scenes. You can use just a part of the background as the whole background for closer shots. This is also helpful in maintaining continuity (as well as saving work).

For 'The Boy Who Cried Wolf', we've created our background key in Flash. You may prefer to rough out your initial drawings on paper. You can then import them into Flash or use them as reference for your Flash version of the same background.

Since we're doing our film in black and white, we've color styled our background with a gray self-color line. This will give our characters with a black outline more contrast when placed over the backgrounds.

We've kept our background fairly simple, but as we'll explain in the animation section, we've divided it up into some separate elements (overlays and underlays) to give it some depth through the pan. We do this by varying the **pan speeds**, giving a sense of perspective.

Designing your backgrounds should be as much fun as animating your film and there are less restrictions since your backgrounds don't have to animate. Here, you can add detail to your drawings without having to worry about moving them around too much.

Color styling

We have already spoken about how color can significantly influence an audience. Color can elicit a strong emotional response and convey mood and atmosphere.

Warm colors can impart a sense of comfort. Cooler colors, a sense of cold or alienation. The color palette used on a character can reflect the character's personality. Bright colors for an extrovert, dark colors for the bad guy. As long as you keep the colors you use consistent they can help the audience identify who the characters are and how they feel about each other. How they fit into the greater scheme of things. All the bad guys could be dressed in light colors, all the good guys in black. The outcast is in a different color palette to everyone else. There are no hard and fast rules.

Once you've rendered a key (establishing shot) background, color style your characters and place them in the shot. This is easy to do in Flash and will give you a good idea of how well they fit into their environment.

Let the colors you use also reflect the time of day. If there is a time change in your film, for example daytime to sunset, adjust the colors accordingly.

Be careful how you use black. Black is not really a color as such. It can sometimes look like a black hole in the screen. Too much black can also make the audience start looking at the surface of the screen rather than the images (your film) projected on it. Don't forget, film is light projected onto a screen. This shouldn't put you off doing that dark, moody opus however. Just be mindful of some of the traps. Be aware of the basic principles. Know the rules so that you can start breaking them!

Over to you

Art direction is all about taking the different visual elements; line, color, design and marrying them to define the look of your film. Addressing these elements in the context of background and character design so each relates to each other and becomes part of a whole. That whole, hopefully, is a film that's great to look at as well as a story that's worth watching.

- Watch the films that you like and be influenced by them. Sometimes this influence is subliminal... seeping in by osmosis. Sometimes it's a little more obvious "I could use that shot!".

- Experiment with different styles and moods to see what happens. It's not too difficult to adjust them if they don't work.

- Explore the different effects that you can achieve with various genres, for example using dramatic lighting for a horror movie.

- Once you have decided upon your film's overall style, stick by your decision. It is important that you resolve all style issues at this stage rather than when the film is half animated.

If handled well art direction is an important part of telling your story and winning the audience over, so time devoted to this now, will enrich your film later.

4: STORYBOARDING

By now you should have a script. In this chapter we'll take its component scenes and look at how best to realize these scenes visually, using good composition and appropriate camera techniques. By the end of this chapter you will be equipped with all the techniques and terminology needed to create your own storyboard.

The storyboard really came into its own with the advent of animated films. In fact, it was the Disney studio that was credited with its invention. Originally called continuity sketches, they were used to illustrate the story in much the same way as a comic does and have continued to be an essential part of the animated filmmaking process.

Laying out a storyboard

As the name suggests, the storyboard should illustrate the story you've written on the page and the film you imagine in your head. This is the first visual representation of your script. At this stage you can work roughly, thinking of the big picture, whilst building the foundations for the more detailed stages that follow. You need to work out how to tell your story effectively, and break your story down into individual shots. Each scene should contain the appropriate dialog and accompanying action.

In professional animation studios this is done by pinning the **board panels** on a wall and presenting them to the director. For our purposes, small, rough drawings, or **thumbnails**, set out on a page will do just fine.

This is the layout of a standard storyboard template as you can see its fairly straght forward.

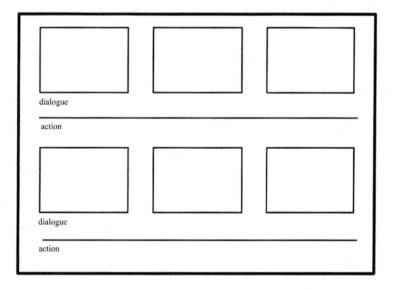

From words to pictures: visualizing your story

It is at the storyboard stage that you begin to develop a strong sense of the way your film will look, thinking practically as well as creatively. Throughout this chapter we'll look at all of the concepts that you will need to consider during this process, from composition and screen direction, to camera movement and what this means in the camera-less environment of Flash. Once you've gained an insight into the terminology and techniques available, then we'll go through our case study to show the decisions that we made creating our storyboard. You will then be equipped to move on to making your own storyboard using everything you have learnt in this chapter.

We'll take a fairly traditional approach to our film, but remember that like any art form, filmmaking encompasses infinite variations. There are no absolutes – no right or wrong way to make a film. The only context in which your film should be judged is whether it is entertaining or not, and even that is highly subjective.

Rules are made to be broken, but in order to break them you first need to know what they are. Throughout this chapter we'll outline the major storyboarding conventions that you need to observe in order to tell your story effectively, and communicate your message to your audience. Once you feel comfortable with some of these do's and don'ts, you can experiment with different approaches, finding your own visual style.

Composition and framing

It's time to consider how to frame your shots; this will have an enormous impact on both the story and the audience. These shots connect characters to their surroundings and to each other as well as helping to tell the story.

Basic shots

These are the ways in which you can frame your scenes. At the most elemental level, they can be broken down into three groups: wide shot, medium shot and close-up. Let's take a look at each one in turn.

Wide shot

Often used as an establishing or opening shot. This is because it connects the character to the background; it shows the audience where they are, where the story is taking place and where the characters are in relation to each other. This is not the only use for wide shots, but be mindful of the fact that a wide shot requires the whole body of the character to be animated and in Flash should be used judiciously!

Medium shot

Can be used when physical acting is required – a hand gesture for example. This type of shot is also good for framing two or more characters.

Close-up

Dialog and more subtle facial expression are best framed in this way. Close-ups also allow us to frame specific actions important to the story, such as a hand picking up a gun, or a foot stubbing out a cigarette.

From these three groups, you can move on to looking at different variations of these basic shots.

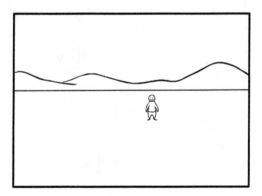

Extreme wide shot

Extreme close-up

Down shot

Up shot

Over the shoulder

One shot

Two shot

Three shot

Flash and the virtual camera

Before we go any further, let's briefly consider the role of the camera in Flash. The use of the camera in filmmaking is crucial – this is the audience's window on events, and our perspective. The camera is used to create drama and tension, to propel the story, and to make the viewer's experience as vivid as possible. This is as true of animated Flash films as it is of Hollywood blockbusters.

In Flash, of course, there is no physical camera, so we need to fake our own 'virtual' camera, which will remain fixed as we move our drawings around it to give the illusion of movement. When we 'zoom in' with Flash we need to make our subjects bigger, rather than moving the camera closer. When we appear to pan across, we are actually moving the background rather than the camera.

We will refer to the camera frequently throughout this chapter – just remember that we mean it in a conceptual way, for instance, if you can visualize where the camera would be in a physical, three-dimensional scene, then this will help you to draw the scene from the appropriate angle. These concepts will become more familiar to you as we start to put them into action in the next chapter. The most important thing to remember is that the camera never moves, the action around it does.

Screen direction

It's important when shooting a film that the audience knows where the characters are in relation to each other (unless they're not supposed to!). For this to be conveyed it is important that we know where the camera is and where we can move the camera in relation to the characters so as not to compromise screen direction and confuse the audience.

Crossing the line

The most fundamental rule of screen direction is the **line of action**, sometimes called the **180° line**. This is an imaginary line that generally runs in front of the camera and marks the boundary of where the camera can be placed without confusing screen direction. To illustrate this, let's look at two characters facing each other.

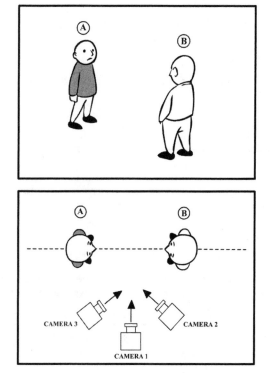

The easiest way to work out where to place the camera is to draw a plan. Here we have placed the camera in three different positions on one side of the line. Let's look at the different shots that will result from these three positions.

Shot one is a wide two shot, taken by Camera 1.

Shot two is a close-up on person A, using Camera 2.

Shot three is a close-up on person B, from Camera 3.

If we ran a sequence using these three camera shots (or **board panels**), then the screen direction is clear – the audience understand exactly where the two characters are.

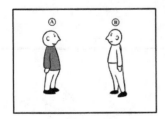

Camera 1   *Camera 2*   *Camera 3*

If, however, we place the camera on the other side of this imaginary line, and replace the third shot with one taken from this angle, then the screen direction appears to be more confusing.

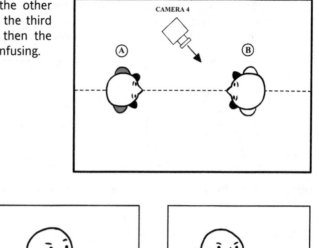

Camera 1   *Camera 2*   *Camera 4*

Character B seems to have mysteriously switched sides as he is now on the left-hand side of the screen, which makes for very disconcerting viewing. Therefore, we can see how important it is to maintain a sense of where the characters are in relation to each other.

Composing the shot

In the previous example, character A is screen left in the first panel. The next panel is a one shot, but he is not placed in the center of the shot, instead he favors screen left. In the last panel, character B favors screen right. When cut together, this will further help the audience understand where the characters are.

Storytelling through composition

The composition of a shot can help the audience understand how the characters are feeling and what their relationship is, as well as where they are physically.

Here, in the first panel, the character is placed centrally. In the second panel, he is placed higher in the shot, which could impart an impression of dominance, strength or threat. Placing the character lower in the third panel suggests the opposite: submissiveness, weakness, or even fear.

When addressing the relationship between two characters, similar rules apply.

In the next example, the first panel shows two characters facing each other. The second is a one shot of the character, screen left. He is quite low in the shot and favoring the left of the screen. The third panel is a one shot of the other character, screen right, who is not only higher in the shot, but also sitting right in the center of the shot. The first character never goes far beyond the left side of the screen, even in a one shot. In contrast the second character owns more of the screen in each of his shots. What does this suggest? Maybe the screen left character is just physically shorter than the other guy. Even so, it also implies that the screen right guy is the dominant figure, especially when coupled with the fact that the first guy is placed over to the left, and the second owning more of the screen.

Positioning alone won't tell the audience the story; rather it helps propel the story in the direction you want it to go, in the light you want it to be seen. In animation time and space are often in short supply, using visual clues can help to convey our story as economically as possible.

Using the camera

By visualizing the key scenes in this way, we've started to think about representing our story graphically, but we need to move beyond this and consider how we can make the most out of the animated medium to bring our story to life. The camera itself can be used to aid the narrative, to create visual interest and to propel the story forward as effectively as possible. Let's see how this is done.

Camera moves

Camera moves add visual interest and give the impression of a world that doesn't stop at the edge of the frame. Camera moves can also be used instead of cutting to another scene. Too many 'hard' cuts can give a choppy look to a film if not used in conjunction with camera moves. In this section we will look at some basic camera moves.

Moving the camera in live action films involves just that: the camera does physically move. This happens whether the camera is fixed and following a moving object by **panning**, or if it's moving with the subject, by **tracking** or **dollying**.

In animation, as mentioned before, the camera is fixed and the drawing is moved, but we retain some of the same live action terms. We still talk about moving or adjusting the camera. In Flash and 3D animation there is, of course, no camera, but just like traditional animation, we need to fake camera moves to give a sense of a real environment.

There are two main camera moves used in animation: pans and trucks. Let's look at these moves now.

Pan

A **pan** is a camera motion that moves across the screen horizontally, vertically or at any angle. In animation, a pan describes what would be a pan or a dolly move in live action.

This is a horizontal pan, covering two fields (screens).

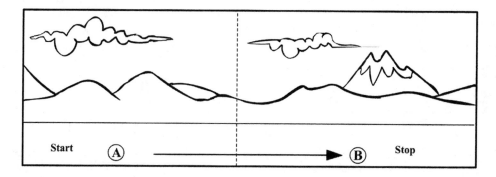

This is a vertical pan, covering two fields.

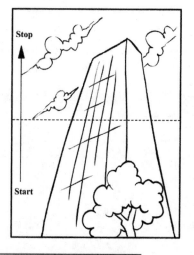

The curved lines used in this shot can help to give an impression of scale.

This is a diagonal pan.

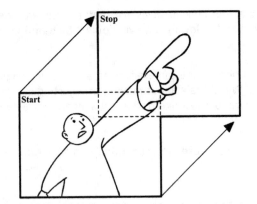

When creating a camera pan in Flash, the principles are much the same as those of the traditional camera. The image itself moves, whilst the camera remains fixed.

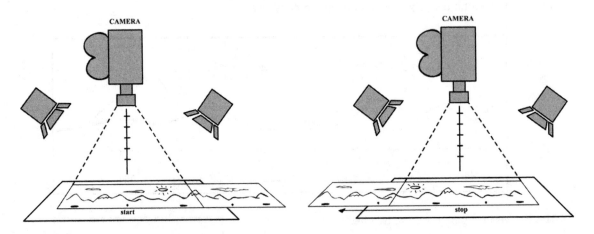

Here we can see the same basic method being used in Flash – the image moves and the camera remains fixed:

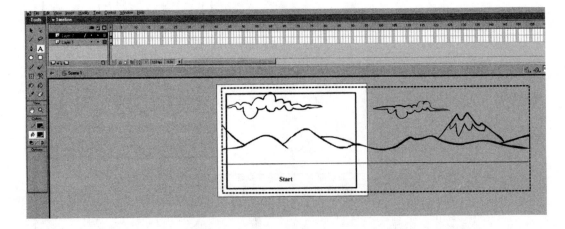

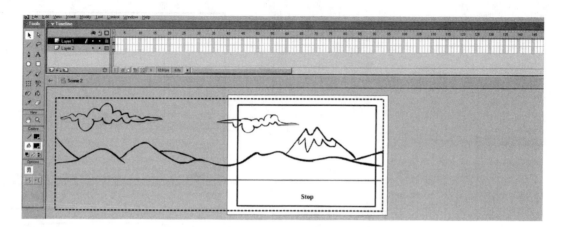

The great advantage of using Flash here is the ability to make instant adjustments to your work.

Truck

A truck is a camera move that makes the shot tighter or wider.

Here we can see a demonstration of a **truck in**, with the camera moving inwards from the start to the stop position.

Conversely, with a **truck out**, the camera starts closer and then moves out.

In traditional animation the truck in represents the camera pushing in on or pulling out from the subject. One of the differences between Flash and traditional animation is the way the camera works. With traditional animation most shots are planned with different **fielding**.

For example, if we were drawing a close up shot, we would not need to draw it to the full size of the paper, we could field it tighter, thus making the drawing itself smaller.

With a wider shot, however, it would be drawn to the full size of the paper allowing for more detail:

Then the camera itself would be adjusted to place the image in field by adjusting the height and focus:

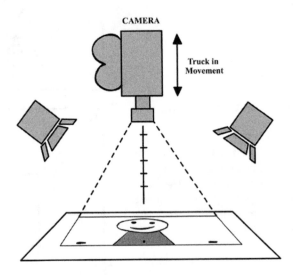

In Flash, the camera works almost in reverse of this situation. The camera remains stationary and the stage is the field of view. Any adjustment to the shot requires changing the dimensions of the image itself, so in this example the image needs to be enlarged:

Flash offers us a lot more freedom when we make camera truck-ins as there are no restrictions on the final field size. We can continue to enlarge the drawing almost endlessly, whereas with a traditional camera there is a limit to how far we can truck in before it just can't get any closer to the image. We have complete freedom to experiment to see what works best and when combined with fades, this can create some very nice effects. We will discuss these in more depth in chapter 5.

Once you're familiar with these camera moves, you can apply them to your basic shots to help tell your story and accommodate the action within.

Using the camera to aid narrative

One important principle is the **establishing shot**. This is used to draw the audience's eye to a certain part of the screen or a certain element in the shot. This then sets the audience up for what is to follow.

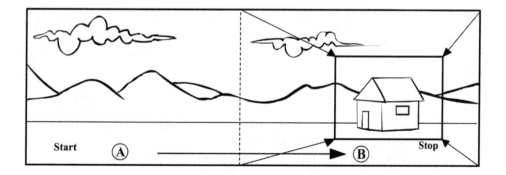

In this establishing shot, the pan sets the scenario and the truck in focuses the audiences attention on the building. This is a very standard shot, which you'll see used in animation and often in film noir style movies.

A camera move can also be used to heighten the drama or tension in a shot.

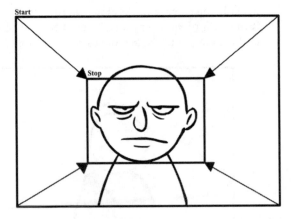

This is a simple shot in which very little happens in the animation, but it can be made quite dramatic by the use of a truck in. Without it, the same shot would seem flat and lifeless.

Music will bring your animations to life too, for instance, a short, tense violin sample added to a truck can really heighten tension. We will cover the addition of sound in more detail in the second part of the Layout chapter.

Using the camera to provide a sense of depth

A moving camera can add another dimension to a shot where you would sometimes have a locked shot. These camera moves are usually fairly subtle, so as not to distract the audience by making them wonder why the camera is moving.

In this scene, the camera moves slowly from the Start to the Stop position, this is a **drift in**. It adds visual interest without impinging on the integrity of the scene. This move would more than likely happen throughout the entire length of the scene, being almost subliminal in its effect, but adding to the drama and tension.

If you animate your characters before you animate camera moves in Flash you will sometimes need to convert your character animation to a seperate symbol that can be tweened at the same speed as the background. More on this in the Layout and Boy Who Cried Wolf chapters.

Drifts can add depth to your film especially when combined with different and separate background and foreground elements. These separate elements are called **overlays** and **underlays**, depending on whether they work in front of or behind the animation. (Overlays in front of the animation and underlays behind.)

To illustrate this, let's look at a sample shot. This wide shot comprises three separate background elements.

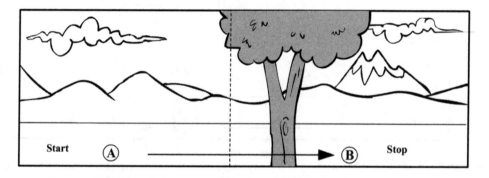

The first element we'll call the **background** – the sky and clouds.

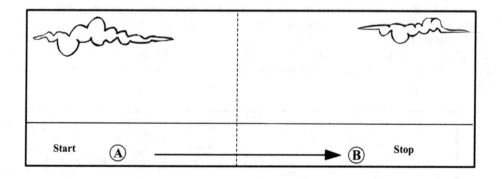

The second, we'll call **underlay** – the distant mountain range and ground plane.

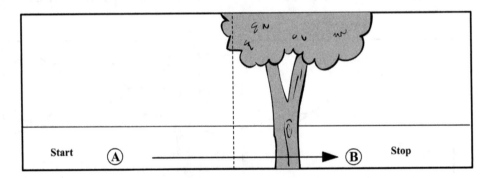

The third is the **overlay** – the foreground tree.

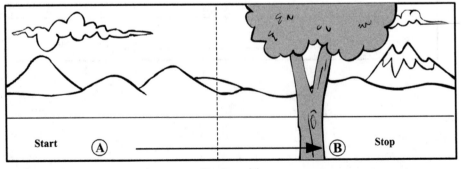

If you pan from position A to position B with all these elements panning at the same speed, the shot will look flat and two-dimensional. No matter how well the background is rendered, it will give little sense of depth.

If you vary the panning speeds of these background elements, you will show real depth and distance and the impression of someone's point of view. In this example, pan the background element very slowly, almost imperceptibly. Pan the underlay a little faster (Note: this will only work if there is no detail on the ground-plane, as any detail would be another element and would need to work within the perspective parameters dictated by the relationship between foreground and background elements). Finally, pan the overlay faster again.

Start position

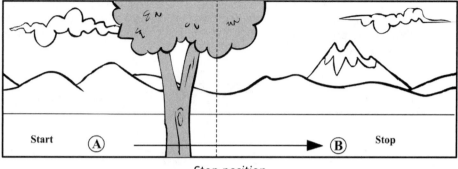

Stop position

This gives you the point of view of someone moving through the shot, like looking out of the window of a moving car – the foreground elements move much faster than those in the distance. We ratio the foreground elements. Ratio refers to moving different elements in a shot at different speeds to give a sense of depth.

Alternatively, try panning the overlay in the opposite direction. This gives the effect of the camera moving around the foreground element (the overlay). The movement of the overlay should be very subtle.

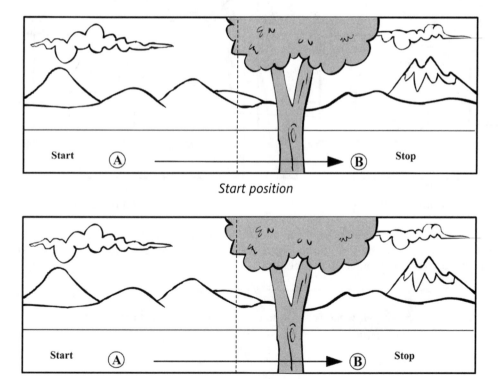

Start position

Stop position

This will give the audience the impression of moving around the tree, creating a very real sense of depth. Don't forget when drawing any background elements that will be panned through the shot that you draw them out far enough to accommodate the move. Make them long enough to allow you the flexibility to adjust the pan speed later on.

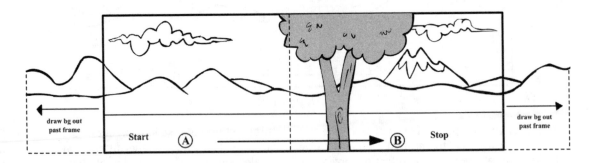

Another effective way to utilize separate elements to give a sense of depth is on a truck in

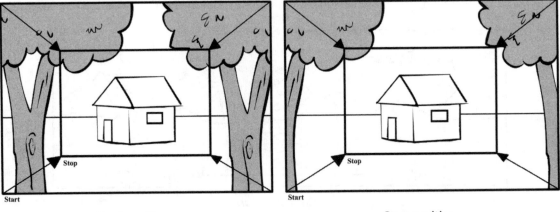

Start position   *Stop position*

As the camera moves in on the house, move the two trees off screen slightly quicker. Again, not only will this add visual interest to the shot, but will give the audience a real sense of moving through the trees and creating a three-dimensional landscape.

> *Don't forget, while there is no actual camera, we are creating the illusion of one.*

What speeds you finally decide on are pretty much a result of trial and error, but requiring little work and resulting in a much more involving scene.

These fundamentals will give you a starting point realizing the camera can be manipulated as much as any animated character in Flash, can save you much work and help tell the story just as effectively.

Using the camera to economize on animation

Since most films animated in Flash are shown primarily on the Internet, it is vital that file size is kept as small as possible. This means limiting the use of full animation so our films can download faster or stream more smoothly. Luckily for us there is a precedent! For years, Saturday morning television animators have been addressing (and in most cases solving) this very problem, and while it is true that there have been some absolutely atrocious shows made in the name of limited animation, the principles on which they are based are sound.

What's more is that animating in Flash offers some distinct (and timesaving) advantages over the traditional 2-D approach, which we'll discuss in more detail in the Flash Animation chapter.

We have to be mindful of telling the story economically through every stage of the filmmaking process. How we frame a shot can help enormously.

In this example we have the character walking, either through shot or center screen (with the background panning). If we take the first approach, shown in image 1, we can use one drawing and using some stretch and squash and motion tweening give the impression of someone walking. Taking the second approach, we have to animate the whole walk cycle.

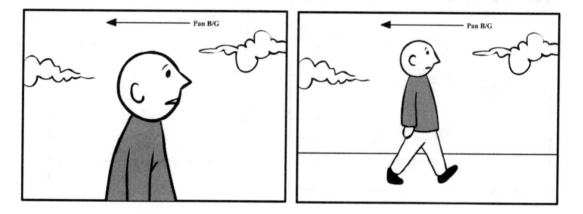

If the film requires a wide shot of the character walking, then it requires a wide shot and all the work that entails, but be mindful of alternatives. How else can I frame this shot? Can it be done another way and still forward the narrative? Some tips of the trade are to design the character in a robe or dress, or to have their legs positioned behind a bush to avoid having to animate the legs.

Another way of limiting animation, championed by Saturday morning TV, is having action happening off screen. Apart from saving work, it is often a more effective way of illustrating a story point.

In this example a character runs centre screen with a panning background. A pole pans into shot and he runs into it.

In this example, the character runs center screen as before. He then starts to gain (gradually starts to move off screen) to the left until he is off screen. Wait a beat (three or four frames at 12fps), then a crash sound effect and a camera shake less work and a more dramatic result.

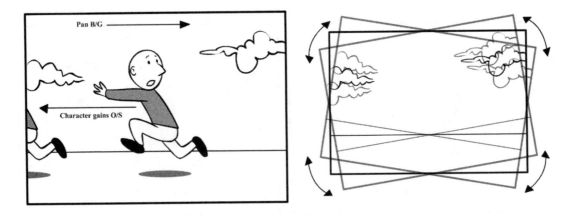

A camera shake is moving the camera around vertically, horizontally or randomly.

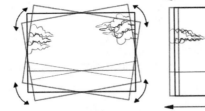
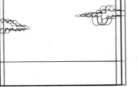
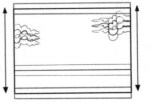

Rotating cam shake   *Vertical cam shake*   *Horizontal cam shake*

Camera shakes aren't quite as effective in Flash as in traditional 2-D animation as we tend to work at 12fps (as opposed to 24fps), but still have their place. Which one you use depends on the action they're describing. For example, someone hitting the ground would require a vertical camera shake as the action is vertical in nature.

Using the camera in Flash often requires little effort (or file size) to add drama, impress the audience and save animation! Amazingly complicated shots executed in live action films can be recreated in Flash. Look closely at how your favourite directors frame shots and move the camera. Guaranteed, it is possible in Flash!

Dissolves, fades and wipes

These are primarily used as a way to represent the passing of time or a move to a different location (or both).

Cross-dissolve

The cross-dissolve can best be described as one scene fading into another. This can be done over any number of frames from, say 6 to 24 (at 12fps). In Flash this is done quite simply by one scene going from Alpha 100% to 0%, while the other goes from 0% to 100%. As we begin to deal with this in the Layout chapter, you'll see the advantages and disadvantages of using this dissolve.

Fade

The fade can be either a fade in or a fade out. Usually (though not necessarily), fade in from black or fade out to black. A fade in following either a fade out or a normal cut can give the impression of being in a completely different time and place. Use a fade when you really want to separate what has come before or what is to follow. A fade in conveys a new stage in the story. In a fade out, you can let the moment sink in before moving on to the next part of the story.

Wipe

There are several different types of wipes. Traditionally a wipe consisted of one scene wiping to another horizontally, vertically, or diagonally, as well as any number of variations.

Horizontal wipe   *Vertical wipe*   *Diagonal wipe*

Wipes aren't often used these days, at least in the above incarnations – even in animation. Another way to wipe from one scene to another is to use something in the shot to motivate the wipe... a foreground element in a pan, or a character moving through shot, bringing the new scene behind them.

In this example, the man moving through the shot in the foreground brings the next scene in behind him. Wipes of this kind (and numerous variations) are making something of a comeback, initially in commercials and now in feature films directed by people who used to make commercials!

Match cut

The match cut is more often than not a dissolve from one scene to another, implying everything a cross-dissolve does. What the match cut adds to the normal cross-dissolve is a very smooth transition visually, by dissolving from one scene to the next where the dominant element (usually) in both scenes share the same place on the screen.

In this example, the sun dissolving to a character's head, offers a basic match cut. The match cut can be taken to another level and become a part of the narrative if the elements of the cut reflect the character involved, or some part of the story. It can then become a humorous element, or an allusion to something in the narrative.

In this example, it's pretty obvious this character is a stooge or victim. Match cuts are a way to really impress your audience, so give them some thought!

Jump cuts

Jump cuts are generally cuts that feel disruptive. They are the opposite of the smoothness and lulling of the audience that we've discussed previously. Time, space, and characters are juxtaposed jarringly. Jump cuts are much in favour as a dramatic device, especially in music videos where style is favoured over narrative. Let's briefly consider some of the pitfalls to avoid.

In the example, we cut from a waist shot of a character to a shot that is slightly tighter. This cut will give the effect of the character 'jumping' towards camera. Be wary of framing shots too similarly, otherwise jump cuts will result.

The Boy Who Cried Wolf

Let's take what we've learned and apply it to the script for 'The Boy Who Cried Wolf'. Already, the script has been refined and condensed. The original story has been broken down into manageable scenes with written cues that are the link between text and what is visually possible. We're now designing the shots, how to compose them and how to link them to produce a cohesive and hopefully, entertaining film.

Scene 1

As the opening shot, we have to involve the audience and set them up for what is to follow. Using a wide, establishing shot, we can connect the boy to his environment. Start on a hill with maybe one sheep, show the title... title fades off and then we pan across to reveal more sheep in the foreground, village in the distance and finally truck in on the boy, sitting under a tree, bored.

Scene 2

Close-up on boy. He shouts to camera " WOLF!!." The close-up imparts a sense of intensity.

Having a character address the camera/audience directly is a device to be used carefully. It can break the illusion of looking into another world, especially if previously they have addressed off-screen characters (each other) by looking past the camera. This is called breaking down the fourth wall – the wall between audience and the stage. In this case it adds to the jarring effect we're after following the languid pace of the opening scene.

Scene 3

Medium shot of villagers panicking (not looking at the camera). A medium shot is good because it's close enough to see how they're feeling, but because it is a group shot it has to be wide enough to include this many characters.

The advantage we have in adapting this fable is that it's so well known. Normally, we'd have to establish where these people are and what their relationship is to the boy. Here we can get away with a reaction shot, and assume that the audience can figure the rest out.

VILLAGERS PANIC - DIAL : "AAGH!!"

Scene 4

Waist shot of the boy. We don't want this shot as tight as Scene 2 because the mood isn't as intense. He's relaxed and smug.

BOY DIAL "JUST KIDDING."

Scene 5

We've used essentially the same setup as Scene 3... maybe slightly wider to impart some lessening of intensity, though the villagers are again reacting to the boy: "Huh?"

We'll then fade to black, indicating that some time has passed.

VILLAGERS: DIAL "HUH?" fade

Scene 6

Hard cut to boy. Now he's even closer than in Scene 2. His head fills the screen.

The closer shot is building the tension. He again shouts (more stridently) "WOLF!!!!!!".

Scene 7

Cut to the villagers, slightly wider again, implying a distancing between villagers and the boy.

They don't know whether to believe him or not. "Really?".

Scene 8

Medium shot of the boy, again smug. Slightly tighter than Scene 4, though nowhere near as tight as the "WOLF!" shots. The mood is still relaxed, though we go tighter to again increase the tension.

Fade to black... time passes.

Scene 9

Extreme close-up on boy (his mouth fills the screen).

Screams "WOLF!!!!!!!". Very intense!

Scene 10

Medium shot of villagers. Framed similarly to Scene 3.

This is emotionally intense for a different reason. Now they're angry!

Scene 11

Start close on the boy with background panning... he seems to be running "Oh no!". Truck out to reveal the wolf chasing him...."AAAAAAAAAAAAAGHHHH!!!".

Cross-dissolve (time passing) to...

Scene 12

Match cut tombstone "RIP The Boy Who Cried Wolf". Truck out to reveal the tree he sat under. Fade on "THE END".

The storyboard as a whole

We've just broken down our storyboard into separate scenes to help explain the shots we've chosen. This is how it looks as complete pages; the scene thumbnails can be as simple as stick figures, or as complicated as slightly better stick figures! The choice is up to you – as long as they get the idea across. The board panels for 'The Boy Who Cried Wolf' are a good example; rough, loose, but telling the story. All that matters is that it makes sense to you. There will be plenty of opportunities later on to impress Joe Public with your considerable drawing skills.

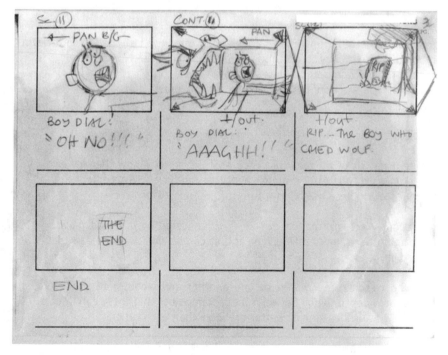

Drawing quality

In the early stages of developing your film, you have to be careful not to waste time or effort on artwork that may or may not be used in the film. Working loosely not only saves time, it also allows you to get your ideas down on paper quickly and encourages you to think more boldly, in a broader and more expansive way.

Conversely, you can also address intricate story/animation problems with any number of sketches, representing ideas, alternatives or solutions with little risk of wasting time and energy. The more polished the drawing, the more time invested, the more reluctant the artist tends to be to let it go even if it is of dubious value in the overall scheme of things. Attachment to a nice illustration can cloud your judgment and vision – you can't see the wood for the trees.

Level of detail

As we have seen, the storyboard is where we first adapt our ideas to some kind of visual representation, and is mostly realized in broad brush strokes. It's big picture stuff. Laying the groundwork for what is to follow. As we move through the following stages we get more and more refined.

In filmmaking, the devil may very well be in the detail, but that's for later on. In the meantime constructing a solid framework can lessen problems in later stages and limit frustrations. What we have here is pretty much what we'll import into Flash, the basis for the next step. Remember, a film is something you build, piece by piece.

Over to you

Now you need to take the script that you developed after the last chapter and begin to sketch out an initial storyboard. The best way to do this is on paper, which you will then scan in to your computer, unless you have access to a drawing tablet, or you are confident of your ability to draw directly onto the computer.

Think about all the concepts that we have looked at here:

- Drawing diagrams of the way that each shot is framed – how the viewer will see things through the camera's eye. This can have a great effect on how much work there will be in future for you on this project.

- Think about what information can be communicated by different pans, trucks, and other camera maneuvers, and of course, what will look good in your film.

- Decide how each scene relates to one another and whether to use cuts, dissolves or wipes to switch between them. Remember that these can impart information as well as looking better or worse than each other.

Your finished work can have as little or as much detail as you feel you need, but as a first-timer, the more planning you do at this stage, the less trouble you may run into later.

5: Layout 1—CREATING AN ANIMATIC

If the storyboard is a loose visual interpretation of the script, then layout is where we refine all the visual elements into a concise and cohesive platform on which we build our film. You should now have your storyboard illustrating each scene of the story by camera movements and shots. In this chapter, we'll work on importing your storyboard into Flash and using it to create a basic animatic, or story reel.

How layout worked traditionally

In traditional 2D animation, the layout department takes the storyboard panels and separates them into individual scenes, putting all the information in scene folders. The layout artist, working with the director will clarify and solve any technical problems. Scenes must be staged accurately, camera moves worked out, and fielding appropriate to what's happening in the scene provided. The layout artist draws up an accurate representation of the background and background elements (overlays, underlays etc.). Characters are drawn to scale and are usually posed in such a way as to describe the main action taking place in the scene.

The layout artist also provides **field guides**, which are used by animators and camera technicians to plot the proportions of artwork to film frame as well as movement and layout, so other departments know how to frame any animation. From here, the background reference goes to the Background department, the animation layouts to the Animation department. All these separate elements come together again in camera, where they hopefully combine seamlessly to produce the scene the director had in mind.

In Flash, the transformation of the storyboard panels into layouts is a lot more basic. We take our board panels and 'cut them up' into individual scenes, building them into a story reel. This is the first version of our film we can actually watch, and serves as the basis for the stages to follow... animation, backgrounds and the rest. We've done our storyboard on paper, so this where we import what we've done so far into the Flash program.

One of the major differences between producing animated films and live action is that some of the procedures performed post-production in live action films are done pre-production in animated films (editing, planning, effects, etc). The nature of animation provides the filmmaker with a lot more control. There is always the opportunity to tweak and refine the film. In live action, a reshoot is a major event, even with all the wonders of CGI!

One great advantage enjoyed by directors of animated films is the ability to view the film shot to length at a very early stage of production, usually cutting the storyboard panels together to provide an **animatic** or Leica reel. This is the first build of the film and as scenes are laid out or animated, they can be cut into the animatic. This animatic lets the filmmaker study the pacing and flow, allowing us to edit as we go and not having to wait until post, though that option still exists.

The Flash advantage

As Flash animators, we have even greater freedom to adjust and refine our film. It's quite easy to make changes and view them immediately rather than wait for film to come back from the lab. Whether 2D or 3D, digital technology has revolutionized how animated films are made and very few studios still employ traditional camera/cell techniques.

We do our layouts within the film itself rather than in folders with information sent off to various departments. As long as the animatic feels right, plays well and the technical problems (like fielding, or camera moves) are addressed, then the layouts are done!

Movie properties

Before we begin making our film in Flash we will need to set the movie properties. This will determine your frame rate and aspect ratio.

Frame rate

Animation and film in general is a series of images placed in front of a camera to create the illusion of movement. How many images or frames we decide to use in a given period of time will affect how smooth the action looks. The **frame rate** is how many frames of film go through the camera in a second.

Traditional film runs at 24 frames per second, video at 25 fps. Flash's default frame rate is 12 fps, and for films made for the Internet, this is the best option as it will stream more smoothly. This works fine as most cartoons made for TV, although shot at 24 frames per second on film, are actually animated at 12 frames per second. Each drawing is exposed for two frames unless a very fast action is required or a camera move is involved, then we use singles (a drawing for every frame).

If you intend to transfer your film to video you may wish to set your frame rate higher – 25 fps is the best option. You will then be able to animate at any frame rate you want, simply holding drawings for two frames will give you the same effect as having your frame rate set at 12 fps. The advantage to working at 25 frames is you will get a much smoother look to your animation, especially with any camera moves, such as trucks and pans. You will eliminate what we call **strobing**, the flickering effect sometimes experienced during these camera moves.

There are also some problems with Flash when you add sounds to films done at 25 fps, as the program can't quite seem to play them in sync properly. So unless you are planning to output your film to video only, stick to 12 fps. It's important to remember that no matter what the frame rate, you do not have to do all those drawings per second. You can hold drawings for as long as you want.

Again, these are techniques perfected in Saturday morning cartoons to save time (and money!) and the same techniques we'll not only address in the Animation section, but embrace wholeheartedly in our quest for entertaining and energy efficient filmmaking.

Aspect ratio

The second thing we need to set is the aspect ratio. **Aspect ratio** describes the width to height ratio of the screen. The aspect ratio is a significant component in defining the look of your film. Whether you want your film to look like a TV show or want a wide screen cinematic effect is determined by the aspect ratio and should be considered in the context of your subject. For example, if your film were a parody of a 50's sitcom, then the aspect ratio would obviously be different to that for an epic western. In traditional filmmaking, there are several different aspect ratios. The two main ones we will be concerned with are:

Standard 4:3

Standard TV has an aspect ration of 4x3 or 1.33:1. In other words, the width of the image is 1.33 times wider then its height and is the same ratio as most computer screens with resolutions equivalent to this ratio e.g. 800x600, 1024x768. This aspect ratio was traditionally used on films made for TV. It is starting to lose favour with the advent of wide screen television and the preference of audiences to see films with bands rather than having the edges cut off for TV.

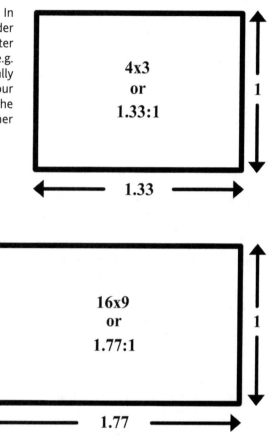

Wide screen 16:9

With the introduction of Digital TV, 16x9 or 1.77:1 is being adopted as the new standard. Even though we refer to this format as 'wide screen', there are wider still, and, are mostly used in feature films.

In Flash, the aspect ratio is described by your document properties and is measured in pixels. This is simply the size of your frame or stage, it is a choice between TV format or wide screen.

For most Internet films, the default Flash ratio of 550x400 is just right, it publishes in the browser window nicely, and no matter what resolution your screen is set on, it should always be in frame. This is probably a good option to start with. Later on you can experiment with different ratios.

If you intend to output your film to video you must set your aspect ratio accordingly.

The following settings are an example of D1 PAL and NTSC Video pixel dimensions (this seems to be the most common), but there are a few things to consider when setting up your movie for transfer to video, most importantly what kind of video editing hardware you intend to use, as this will effect the way you need to set your movie dimensions in Flash. We recommend you research your video transfer options before starting your movie if you intend to output your film to tape.

D1 PAL

- **Standard 4:3** – 720 x 576 (pixel aspect ratio 1.07)
- **Wide screen 16:9** – 720 x 576 (pixel aspect ratio 1.42)

D1 NTSC

- **Standard 4:3** – 720 x 480 (pixel aspect ratio 0.9)
- **Wide screen 16:9** – Wide screen = 720 x 480 (pixel aspect ratio 1.2)

Another thing to consider (and this is something a lot of people misunderstand) is that Flash creates images in square pixels, and videotape has rectangular pixels. So setting your pixel dimensions in Flash the same as the video dimensions above will create a slightly stretched image when transferred to tape. It is therefore best to set your movie dimensions in square pixels, then convert the images to the video dimensions for transfer to tape after outputting from Flash – again, this will depend on your video editing hardware.

The square pixel dimensions for the above video aspect ratios should be created at:

- **Pal square pixel** – 768 x 576
- **NTSC square pixel** – 720 x 540 (as shown in the broadcast template in Flash, see this mentioned below)

Setting your aspect ratio properties

To set these properties, open Flash, and then expand the Property inspector at the bottom of the screen. Clicking on the Size tab will bring up the Document Properties window.

The default settings are Dimensions at 550 x 400 and Frame Rate at 12 fps. If you want to use an aspect ratio, or frame rate other than the default one, adjust the figures here as required.

Once you've done this, save your movie.

Go to File > Save, select your path (where you will save it) name your movie. In this case we're calling it animatic. Then click Save.

> Remember to save your work often, there's nothing more likely to lead to alcohol abuse than having to reanimate something because of a computer crash.

TV cut off

The area of your stage that you can be pretty sure will be seen on the audience's TV or monitor, is described by the TV cut off. This is where the edge of the TV screen will be. Since the TV frame is not the exact same dimensions as the stage, there will always be a part of the image lost in the transfer to video.

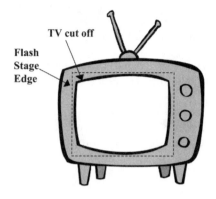

In traditional animation, artists try to keep important action or acting within this area. You don't want anything significant happening right at the edge of the screen, otherwise it might end up happening off screen!

We can see that although this shot seems fine on the stage, once it is transferred to video, the amount of the image that will be lost in the transfer makes the shot unclear and a lot less effective.

If you're only making your film for the Internet, this is not really a concern. If however, you intend at some point to output it to video, then you should keep this in mind, as it will eliminate a lot of annoying resizing later on.

It is helpful to draw a frame inside the main stage area, which will ensure that all your action will take place within the field of view. This i known as a **field safe guide** or **TV safe guide** and should be placed on a seperate layer.

We will make a field guide for our animatic. It's important to note here, that since we are making this film for the Internet only and with no intention of exporting it to video, we are going to make our field guide as a reference guide only and will mainly be for helping to align our storyboard panels when we import them, (this will become clearer as we progress.)

The actual area you can lose with video transfer can vary quite a lot and this guide should be made about three grid spaces inside the stage as opposed to the one grid space guide we'll be making.

Flash MX users should note that this version now comes with a TV safe guide template, ready to use. To access this template select File >New From Template >Broadcast. This will open a new movie with a field guide already drawn for you. You can then scale the template to suit your movie.

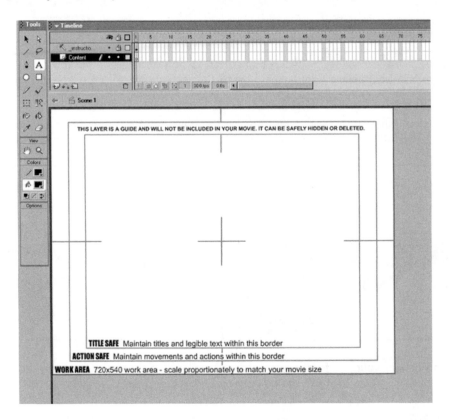

You'll notice three frames in this template, the inner one is labeled Title Safe; this is your minimum image area for any titles or fonts. The second is the Action Safe frame; this is where all the important actions should take place.

We will not use this template to make our guide, as our film is destined purely for the Internet – we'll be using our field guide mainly to align our storyboard panels.

Using the grid

To draw your field guide, first turn on your grid, by clicking on View > Grid > Show Grid (or CTRL/⌘ + #.) Flash will now place a grid on the stage. This is a very useful tool for placing objects and characters on the stage,and aligning artwork – we'll be using it quite often in the chapters to follow. The default grid size is 18 x 18 pixels, and this is the one will we use here.

We need to label this layer. Double-click on the layer name (Layer 1), and then label it 'TV Frame'.

> *You should get into the habit of naming all your layers; it will make things a lot clearer and easier to work with especially when we get into animation. You will find that you will use a lot of layers and it's easy to get lost if the layers are just named numerically.*

Now to set our TV cut off. With frame one selected, choose the Rectangle tool from the main tool bar.

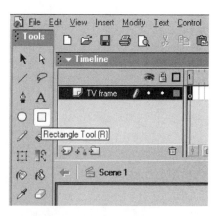

Then select a color for the frame – red works well for this as it stands out from other line work.

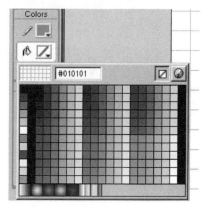

To set the width of this line, go to the Property inspector at the bottom of the screen, then choose a width with the slide control. In this case we used 2, which is wide enough to be easily seen.

Next select the fill color as transparent; this is the small square tab with a red line through it on the right-top side of the color selector.

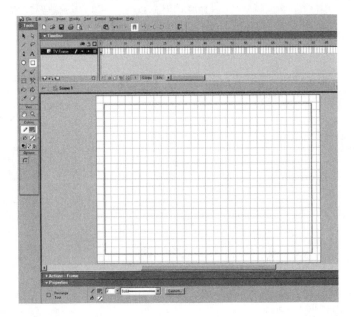

Then draw your frame, about one square on the grid inside the stage edge. This will give you a guide to keep all your animation inside without significantly eating into your stage area. As well as being mindful of not losing animation at the edge of the screen, you don't want all the action happening in the centre with a lot of empty space around it.

Since we are making this film with no intention of outputting it to video, we are setting up this field guide only as a reference guide. The actual area you can lose with video transfer can vary quite a lot. The best bet is to make your TV cut-off further in from the stage edge – 2.5-3 grid spaces inside is a safe guide.

Creating layers

Traditional animation is shot under the camera in different levels or layers. Each level contains a different element. For example, one level for the background, another for the first character, and yet another for the second character. This gives the animator the freedom of moving, or timing each level independently of each other.

In limited animation, characters are broken down into separate elements such as body, head, mouth and so on. To work most effectively, it is best to think about it at the art direction stage, as we have done. We'll really get into the detail of this in the Flash Animation chapter, but here we need to learn the basic mechanics of layers so we can import the storyboard.

One of the advantages of Flash is that, unlike traditional **cel animation**, you are not limited with the number of layers or (levels) that you can use. With traditional animation, all the drawings are copied onto clear acetate cels, so there is a limit to the amount of these you can place on top of each other before you begin to get shadows or slight color changes. Since Flash eliminates the cells, it also eliminates these inconsistencies, giving us the advantage of unlimited layers. With this said however, most traditional animation these days is being painted and shot in different compositing programs, and possibly it's only a matter of time before the use of cels is completely outdated.

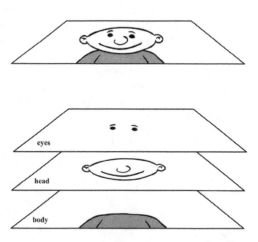

To create layers in Flash, click on the Insert Layer tab in the bottom left-hand side of your timeline, then label it. As this will be the layer we will import the storyboard to, label it 'Storyboard'.

If you had the TV Frame layer selected when you added this new layer, you will notice that Flash has placed the new layer on top of the TV Frame level. Since we want this layer under the TV Frame, simply click on the layer then drag it below. You'll find that you will need to move layers around quite a lot, especially when we start animation.

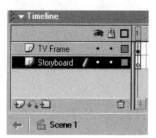

Importing the storyboard

The transition from storyboard to layout stage isn't as involved as in traditional animation. The layout in Flash is little more than the storyboard panels made into individual scenes and roughly timing them so we have a film that we can play back, watch and refine. In traditional animation, the layout artist redraws all the elements in much greater detail – staging the shots, drawing up the background elements and providing main character poses for the animator. With Flash, we put all these elements straight into our film and build it from there.

Since we have done our storyboard on paper, we will be scanning our drawings then importing them into Flash. As with most things in animation there are no hard and fast rules and in some situations it might prove just as easy to draw everything directly into Flash. Drawing your board on paper, especially when new at animating in Flash, allows you to concentrate on the story rather than getting bogged down in the mechanics of illustrating your ideas.

It's helpful at this stage if you can take the storyboard and 'cut out' and save each panel individually. JPEG or GIF images work well for this as they are small in size. Two good third-party programs for this are Paintshop Pro or Adobe Photoshop. If you don't have access to these programs, don't worry you can still achieve the same effect.

> *Be sure to name all your images in sequence before importing them. This will help keep everything organized as we proceed, for example sb panel 01, 02, 03 etc. It's always best to start labeling things with an initial zero, such as 01, so that when you get to image 10, things don't get all mixed up.*

Now we're ready to start importing our storyboard images. Each image or frame represents a separate scene or action within a scene. What we're creating is a cartoon strip that we can play back as a story. It's a platform onto which we build our film - this will become our **animatic**.

Select frame one of the Storyboard layer, then click on File > Import or Ctrl/⌘ + R, select the files to import, and then click Open.

> *If you've labeled your images in sequence, you need only select the first one; Flash will then ask you if you'd like to import the entire sequence, click* Yes.

Flash has now placed all the images on the timeline and in the Library, with the first frame visible on the stage. The first storyboard panel for 'The Boy Who Cried Wolf' looks like this on the stage, each separate image is placed on its own frame:

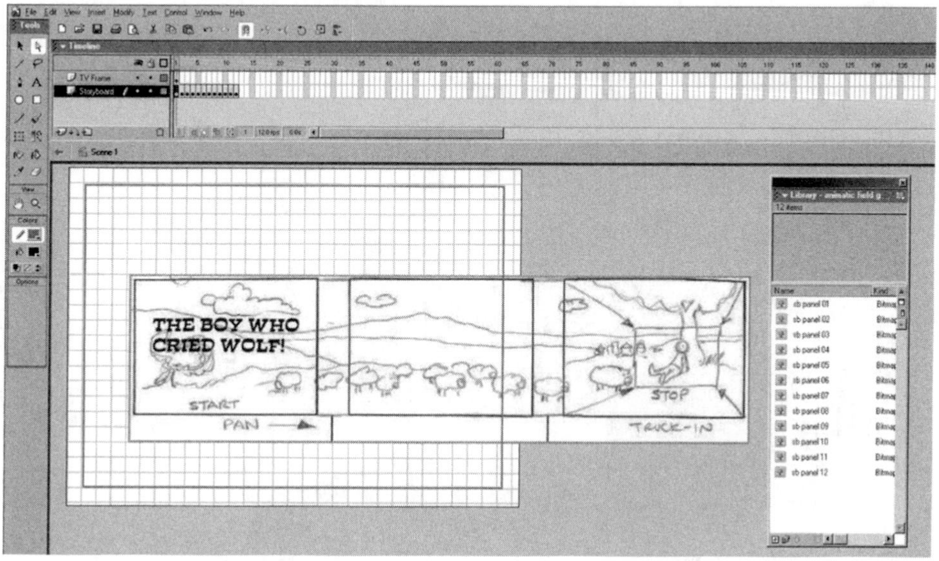

If you were not able to cut out the images separately, it just means that you will have imported the entire page, and it will be a little more difficult to manipulate the image.

Another benefit of having smaller images is that Flash will be able to play them a bit more smoothly when we come to testing our animatic (story reel). But it really won't make that much difference, we'll be replacing the storyboard panels later on, and it's mainly for convenience.

Scaling the storyboard panels

Here we begin composing our individual scenes. Taking our storyboard panels and fitting them into our field guide on the stage. Keep in mind the TV cut offs and how well centred the board panel is. Like everything else in Flash, you can always adjust it again later on but it's a good idea to keep composition in mind, even at this early stage.

Select your first image by clicking on it either in the timeline or on the stage. The frame you've selected will be highlighted in your timeline and will have a dotted line around it on the stage.

Select the Transform tool from the toolbar, and then select the Scale tool.

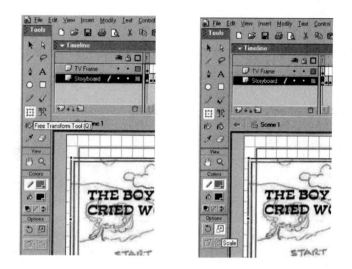

Now grab one of the corner edges and drag the drawing to fit the frame by holding down on it – with the Arrow tool you can move it anywhere in the frame. You will find the field guide useful here, resize the image to match it.

> Be sure to grab one of the corner handles of the image as this will perform a scale operation that keeps the same ratio of width to height. If you grab any of the middle handles, the image will resize by either stretching up or across.

This kind of resizing is very useful and we'll go into that later. For now, we just want to resize the image, keeping the same proportions.

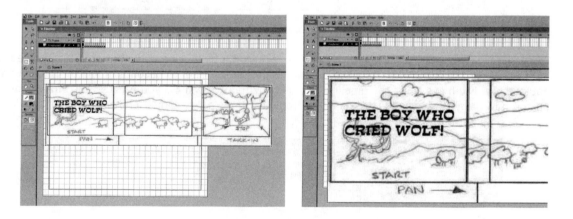

Since this opening scene is a pan, with more than one panel illustrating the scene, we will just center the first frame of the scene for now – and move on.

Adding and deleting frames

As this is Scene 1 and we only want the first storyboard image, we can delete the others from the scene. Adding and deleting frames is often done in the context of animating and animation timing as you tweak your scenes.

In the timeline, select the other images by clicking, holding down and moving along the timeline. Once all the frames are selected go to Insert > Remove Frames or SHIFT + F5. This will delete all the other frames.

We don't want this scene to be one frame long. We need to have each scene long enough to watch when we play it back. So now we need to add frames.

The exact length of the scene is not really important at this stage so we'll start with 50 frames as a rough guide. We will adjust this later as the film begins to take shape and we start thinking about the pacing and how our film cuts together and plays back.

To add frames, move across to frame 50 then select the frame on both layers. Then click Insert > Frame or F5. Our scene is now 50 frames long.

You easily can check your scene length in frames or in seconds by looking at the bottom of your timeline. In this instance, the scene is 50 frames at 12 frames per second and 4.1 seconds in length. You will also notice that if you move along the timeline or select any frame it will tell you exactly which frame you're on and how many seconds into the scene that frame is. This is particularly useful when animating.

Creating scenes

Since the storyboard is divided into separate scenes, the next step will be to create these scenes in Flash, then insert and scale the storyboard panels into each of these scenes the same as we have with Scene 1.

Creating separate scenes allows you to organize the entire movie into more manageable sections. This is also how films are traditionally made, with each new shot, a new scene. You may find that as you start testing your work, you need to change the order of these scenes – having them grouped separately makes this a lot easier. This is normally the job of the editor and in live action is done in post-production.

To create a new scene, click on Insert > Scene. Flash has now created a new, empty Scene 2.

We now need to place the storyboard image for Scene 2 into it. Since all the storyboard images are in the Library we simply need to drag it into the scene and resize it as we did with Scene 1
To do this, open the Library by clicking on Window > Library.

Then select the image from the Library for the second storyboard panel, click on it, and drag it onto the stage, then extend the scene to 50 frames exactly as we did in Scene 1.

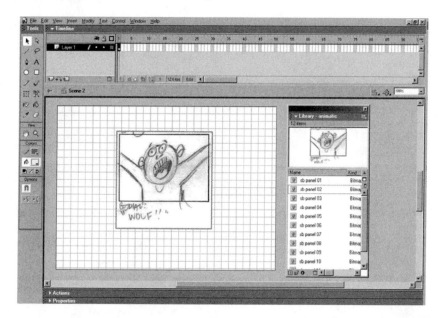

To add the TV frame cut off, return to Scene 1 by going to the scene selector on the bottom right-hand side of your timeline, then select Scene 1.

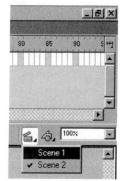

Then in your timeline for Scene 1, select the first frame of the
TV Frame layer and copy it,
Edit > Copy Frames or CTRL/⌘ + ALT + C.

Then use the scene selector to go back to Scene 2, insert a new
layer, select the first frame, and paste the TV frame in. Edit >
Paste Frames or CTRL/⌘ + ALT + V.

You'll notice that Flash has also renamed the layer and added the appropriate amount of frames. Enlarge
the image to the size of the TV frame, the same as we did with Scene 1.

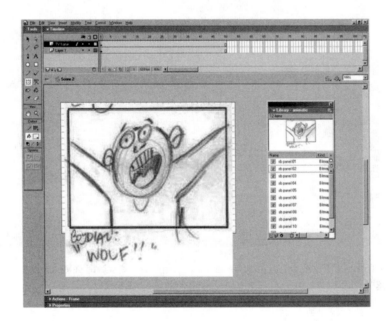

Follow the same steps to set up all the remaining scenes in your storyboard. This is how this looks for 'The Boy Who Cried Wolf'.

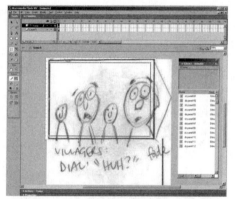

As in Scene 1, there is more than one panel to describe the action in Scene 11. Just use the first panel for now.

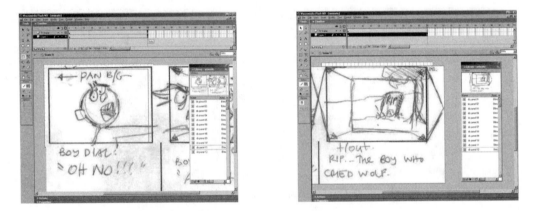

We have now created all the scenes in the movie and have laid out the basic structure of the animatic. We now have a story reel we can play back, it won't be very interesting to look at, or have any animation in it, but the basic structure of our final animation is already in place.

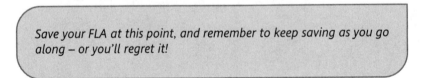

Save your FLA at this point, and remember to keep saving as you go along – or you'll regret it!

We can now start the process of refining the animatic, and we'll use the storyboard panels to set up the camera movements. Remember that our 'camera' in Flash behaves differently to a real camera – it stays the same and the pictures change.

Creating a pan

The first scene in our movie involves a pan, and that's a good place to start. As we just discussed, creating a pan simply involves moving the image from one position to another under the camera.

In Scene 11 of our film, we have an example of another kind of pan (technically it's a dolly shot), which is basically a variation on a theme. The background moves through the shot while the boy, and the wolf, remain center screen – but more of that later!

We have already set up Scene 1 with the first position, so our next step is to create the final position. Then tell Flash how to move between the two.

Before we can reposition the storyboard panel and move it from one position to the next, we will need to convert it to a symbol so that Flash can understand it then manipulate it.

Converting images to symbols

Converting images to symbols will be one of the most important and widely used functions in animating with Flash and we'll discuss it again and in more detail in the following chapters.

There are three different types of symbols: graphic symbols, button symbols and movie clip symbols. The one we will be most concerned with is the graphic symbol,. Basically, a graphic symbol is a static image that is saved into the Library by converting an existing image, as in this case, or by creating it from scratch (drawing it in Flash).

To convert an existing image to a symbol, select the image on the stage or in the timeline, in this case the storyboard image in Scene 1. Then select Insert> Convert to Symbol or hit F8.

Flash will then prompt you to name and select a type of symbol. In this case we'll call it 'storyboard panel 1' and make it a graphic symbol.

If you are using Flash MX, you will also notice a Registration selection image in the dialog box, by default Flash will place it in the center and for our purposes, this is just what we want, so click OK.

If you're using an earlier version of Flash, the center will always be the default – although in any version you can alter it later if need be.

We have now converted this image to a graphic symbol, and it has been placed in the Library. We can now start to create our first pan.

Layer control

Before we begin creating our first pan, let's take a quick look at the timeline and the different ways that you can control the layers. You'll notice that on the top left-hand side of your timeline there are three different icons: an eye, a padlock and a square.

These control how the layer is viewed and whether it can be edited or not.

- The first icon, the eye, is the show/hide all layers selector and when selected will make the layer invisible on the stage, it will also mean that the layer cannot be edited while selected. This is very useful and we will discuss this in more detail in the Animation chapter.

- The second icon, the lock, the one we will be concerned with now is the lock/unlock all layers selector and when selected will lock the layer but still leave it visible. This means that although we can still see the layer, we will not be able to edit or move the image in this layer.

- The third icon, the square, is the show all layer outlines selector and is similar to the onion-skinning function and we will discuss this in the animation chapter when it will really come into play.

Creating this pan will involve moving the position of the storyboard layer, if we lock the TV Frame layer, it can't accidentally get moved while we are re-positioning the storyboard panel. So, in the layer for the TV Frame, click on the dot below the lock - another lock will appear by that layer name, indicating that the layer is locked, and the TV frame cannot be moved.

You'll notice that if you click on the lock itself it will lock all the layers. The same applies with the other two icons.

As our first scene is the establishing shot and our first frame contains our titles, we will want to hold on this frame for a while before we start our pan. As we discussed before, the exact length of this scene will be adjusted later as we begin to test our animatic. For now, we just need to set up the mechanics of the scene.

Starting to pan

As the first panel is held for 50 frames, we will want to insert another 50 frames for the pan. Again, the time we've chosen is totally arbitrary and just a place to start.

Since the pan will start on frame 50, we need to insert a keyframe for the storyboard layer here so that flash will know where to start the pan. Keyframes represent key points of reference in animation, or any kind of action (such as camera moves).

Insert a keyframe, select frame 50 of the storyboard layer then select Insert > Keyframe (F6):

Flash has now placed a new keyframe in the timeline.

Now go to frame 100, then select the frame for both layers and insert new frames as we did previously. Insert > Frame (F5).

The length of our total scene is now 100 frames, with a keyframe on frame 50 of the storyboard layer where the pan will start.

Next we need a stop position for the pan, so insert a new keyframe at frame 100 of the storyboard layer, exactly as we did on frame 50. We now have our start and stop positions on the timeline.

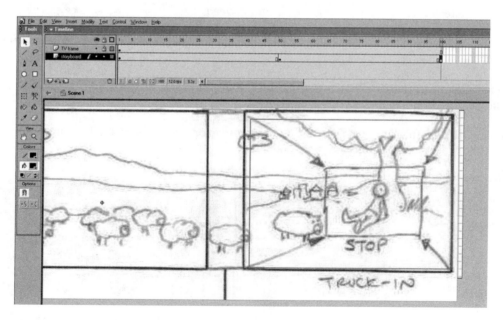

Next we want to reposition the storyboard on frame 100 to place the final panel in field.
To do this, select the Arrow tool.

Then click on the storyboard image on the stage or select it in the timeline. A blue outline should appear around the image.

By clicking and holding down on the image, you should now be able to drag it anywhere on the stage. Drag it across and position the last panel so that it is in frame (the TV cut off will be useful here.)

Holding down SHIFT while click-dragging will restrict the movement, helping to maintain horizontal alignment.

We now have our start and stop positions.

Another way to move images around is to use the arrow buttons on your keyboard. Simply select the image and press the key in the direction you want to move the image. This is very useful when accuracy is required, as the image will move on the exact same axis as the key you are selecting. Dragging images with the Arrow tool is very handy but not as exact as using the keyboard.

The next step is to tell Flash to move between the two positions.

Tweening basics

Motion tweening is one of the cornerstones of animating in Flash. In traditional animation, this is what is known as **in-betweening** (more in the Animation Principles chapter) and in Flash is simply moving an object from one position to another.

As we discussed before, this can only be done with images that have been created as, or converted to symbols.

To illustrate, in this situation we have a static image in two different positions and we want Flash to create the images, or tweens, between these two positions.

Keyframe 1   *Motion tweens*   *Keyframe 2*

This is exactly what Flash will be doing with our storyboard image, creating the tweens between our two keyframes.

To tell Flash to create these motion tweens, select the start position storyboard panel on frame 50 of the timeline, then select Insert > Create Motion Tween.

You can also do this by expanding your Property inspector dialog box at the bottom of the screen and selecting the Tween box, then selecting Motion.

You can now see that Flash has placed an arrow in the storyboard layer between our start position and our stop position in the timeline. This means that all the tweens between these two positions have been successfully created.

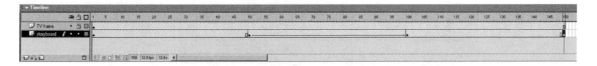

To check this, click and hold down on the red frame indicator on the top of the timeline and move the cursor along the scene. You should be able to see the storyboard moving from one position to the next.

Our first pan is done. Save your work!

As we discussed previously there are different kinds of pans. The one we've just created is a horizontal pan, but the principles are the same for them all whether they are horizontal, vertical or diagonal. It's simply a matter of moving from one position to the next.

There are, however, a lot of variables and most are related to timing, which we will discuss in more detail when we get to the main Flash Animation chapter.

Creating a camera truck

Now that we have created our pan and the final position of the scene is at the end position of our storyboard panel, the next step is to create our truck in. This involves us pushing in on the character sitting under the tree. As we said previously, with Flash it's not the camera that will zoom in, but the scene that will enlarge to fill our stage.

To do this, we will follow exactly the same steps as we did to create the pan – with one difference.

Since the last frame of the pan will become the first frame of the truck in, what we need to do next is create the final position of the truck in.

We'll also make the truck in 50 frames for now just to keep everything even. So go to frame 150 in the timeline, then insert frames the same way we did for the pan, then create a keyframe for the final position of the truck in on frame 150. Your timeline will now look like this:

Depending on the size of your monitor, you may not be able to view all the frames in your timeline at this point, so you may need to scroll along to frame 150. To do this, hold down on the bar at the bottom of the timeline, next to the seconds counter, and move it across to the right. This will move the timeline along to the required position.

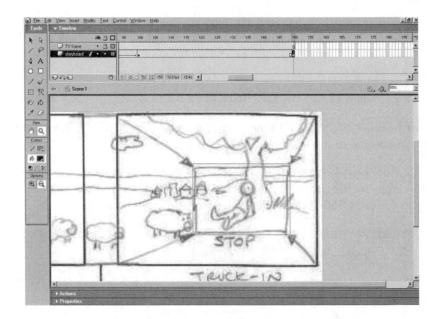

We now have our start and stop positions for the truck in, with the final position of the storyboard on frame 150. Select this. We now need to enlarge the panel so that the final truck position fills the stage.

Do this the same way that we enlarged the image when importing and resizing our storyboard, with the Transform and Scale tools. You may need to move the image slightly (with the Arrow tool or the keys) to set it central within the TV safe frame.

With the TV frame the same as the final truck position on the storyboard., the final frame should now look like this:

The tweening function not only tweens images of the same dimensions, but can also create tweens of images that change in size as well. So all we need to do now is to tell Flash to motion tween our truck in keyframes the same as we did with the pan.

Select the start position keyframe of the truck in on frame 100, then select Insert > Create Motion Tween and "Hey presto!" our truck in is done. Flash has added another arrow between the two keyframes indicating that the tweens have been created.

You can check it the same way we did with the pan by moving along the timeline with the cursor.

As with the pan, we will refine all the timing when we get to animation, but for now the first scene in our animatic is done. This is a good time to save your work.

Transitions

We have now covered the basics of pans and camera trucks. The next topic to cover is **fades and cross-dissolves**. As we discussed in the storyboarding chapter, these are camera effects used mostly to represent time passing, or transitions between scenes.

Fades and dissolves are created by reducing or increasing an image's **transparency**, also known as its alpha value. For example, if an image's alpha value is set at 100%, the image is totally opaque, and if it is reduced to 0% then the image becomes totally transparent.

Therefore, to fade an image off, we would start its alpha value at 100% then over time reduce it to 0% – the image would then appear to disappear, or fade off, and in reverse would appear, or fade on.

A wipe is where one scene moves across camera following a line either vertical horizontal or diagonal to fill screen. There are other forms of wipes as well that you, dear reader, will have to discover for yourself. Generally speaking, wipes (another type of transition) are something to be avoided in Flash as they're difficult to achieve. In live action, wipes had been out of favour for quite a while, but seem to be making something of a comeback.

Creating a fade

Since the most common type of fade is a fade to black and the fade that we will be using in our film, let's start here.

As we just discussed a fade is simply reducing or increasing an images alpha value over time from 100% to 0%, or reverse depending on whether it is a fade in or a fade out.

We want to have our image fade to black, and as our stage background color is set to white, simply reducing the images alpha value to 0% will leave us with a totally white frame. So the best way to achieve this fade is to create what we call a **black matte** that will cover the entire stage area including our animation, and increase its alpha value from 0 to 100%, turning the entire scene black.

> *There are also problems in Flash with fading off images that are animating, especially when we have separate levels – so this is a good work-around.*

The first fade in our film is in Scene 5. The first thing we will need to do is to create a new level for the black matte. As this level needs to be on top, select the TV frame layer, then add a new layer on top of that and label it 'black'

Since we want to start the fade at the end of the scene, we will need to create a keyframe for the matte on frame 50, then extend the scene to accommodate the fade – 25 frames will do for now.

To create the matte, select frame 50 in the black layer and draw a rectangle exactly as we did for the TV frame, only instead of making the fill area empty, select black and draw it so it covers the entire stage area.

Then convert the image to a symbol, Insert > Convert to Symbol (or F8), name it 'black matte'. If you forget to covert your black rectangle into a symbol, the tween won't work, and you'll be unable to create the fade.

Next create a new keyframe on frame 75, these will be the start and stop positions of the fade. As we want this matte to fade on, the next step is to reduce the alpha value of the start position to 0%. Select the matte by clicking on it on the stage, then, expanding the Property inspector if need be, in the drop-down menu next to Color, select Alpha.

Then select the slide control to the right and move it to 0%, you will notice on the stage as you move the slide control, the image's transparency will change and you will be able to see the storyboard underneath it.

We now have our start position on frame 50 at 0% and our stop position at frame 75 at 100%.

By creating motion tweens between the two keyframes, exactly as we did with the pan and the truck in, Flash will now create the tween states that will increase the alpha value over the 25 frames at the end of the scene. To check this, move the cursor along the timeline and you can see the scene fading to black.

> *Since we are going to do exactly the same fade in Scene 8 you can copy and paste the fade from here.*

Simply highlight frames 50 to 75 in the black layer, and then select Edit > Copy Frames (CTRL/⌘ + ALT + C). Go to Scene 8, add a new layer extending the scene to 75 frames, insert a keyframe on frame 50, then paste the fade. (Edit > Paste Frames or CTRL/⌘ + ALT + V).

The fade has now been added to Scene 8.

Creating a cross-dissolve

A cross-dissolve is when a scene fades out as the following scene fades in over the top. Creating a cross-dissolve in Flash is much the same as creating a fade, only that instead of the scene fading to black, the scene will fade out to an alpha value of 0% and at the same time the following scene will fade on to 100%.

As we said when creating a fade, there are problems in Flash associated with this kind of camera effect and they will be discussed in the Animation chapter but for now since we just need to dissolve between two held images, these won't be a concern.

You'll notice on the storyboard that not only is there a cross-dissolve between Scenes 11 and 12 but there are also two trucks and a background pan.

The background pan in Scene 11 is not of concern to us at this point, so we won't worry about that until we get to the Animation chapter. The first truck out in Scene 11, however, will need to be dealt with now, before we start on our cross-dissolve, so go to Scene 11 and create the truck out as follows.

Dissolve set-up, first a truck

Since the first panel in Scene 11 is the same as the start position of the second panel, there is really no need, for the purpose of our animatic, to use both, so we will reposition and enlarge the second panel of the scene to use as our start position.

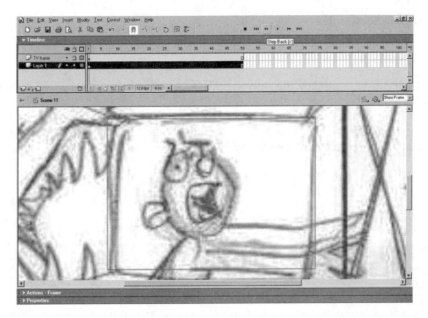

Extend the scene to 100 frames, then convert the storyboard image to a symbol, add keyframes on frames 50 and 75.

Next enlarge the final position on frame 75 to match the TV cut off and insert motion tweens between the two to create the first truck out.

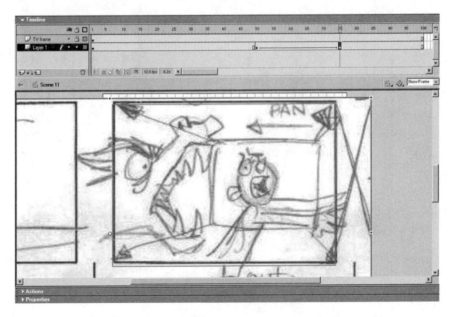

Now things get a little tricky, but it's not that hard when you've got the hang of it.

Combining scenes to dissolve

Since it's not possible to create a cross-dissolve between two separate scenes in Flash, we are going to need to combine the two scenes.

Firstly go to Scene 12, and copy the storyboard layer exactly as we did when we copied the fade from Scene 5 to Scene 8.

Then go back to Scene 11, add a new layer, extend the scene to 150 frames, insert a new keyframe at frame 100, and paste the frames from Scene 12 to the new layer in Scene 11 at frame 100.

It's best to label your layers. We'll call them 'sc11' and 'sc12'. Your timeline in Scene 11 should now look like this:

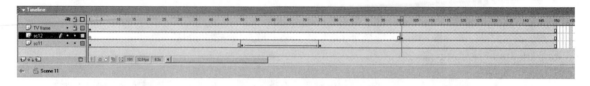

Enlarge the storyboard panel for sc12 so that the truck start position is in frame.

As with any camera move, we will need to establish our start and stop positions. So on frame 100, create a start position for the truck in layer sc11 by inserting a keyframe at frame 100. Then create a stop position for both layers on frame 125.

The cross-dissolve

A cross-dissolve involves fading out one image and fading in the other. Since we want sc11 to fade out, go to the final position on frame 125 in that layer and adjust the alpha value to 0%, as we did with the fade.

Then since we want sc12 to fade in, go to the start position of that layer and adjust the alpha value to 0%. We now have our start and stop values.

To save on the processing power required for this fade, you could choose to just fade in the upper layer, the lower layer will naturally be obscured as the higher one becomes opaque. This will reduce your overall file size, as Flash doesn't work as hard to render this effect.

Next, simply create motion tweens between the two positions in each layer. And that's it! The cross-dissolve is done. You can check it, as before, by sliding your cursor along the timeline.

Another way of creating motion tweens is to select the frame you want, then click the right mouse button (or CTRL-click on the Mac) to bring up the context menu, and select Create Motion Tween.

You can also create motion tweens on several layers at once by highlighting all the start positions on the separate layers and then selecting Create Motion Tween. *This will be really handy when we start animation.*

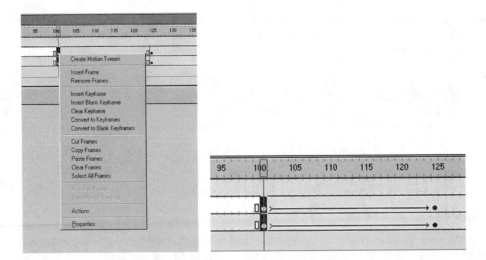

Completing the animatic – fade to black

With our cross-dissolve done, all that remains to complete our animatic is to add the final truck out and fade to black.

Firstly, extend the Scene 11 by 50 frames to make it a total of 200 frames long.

Next go to frame 200 and insert a final position for the truck out in Scene 12. Resize the storyboard panel and create motion tweens to complete the final truck out.

We've made this truck out longer as it's the final scene of the show and we will also need to incorporate the fade to black over it.

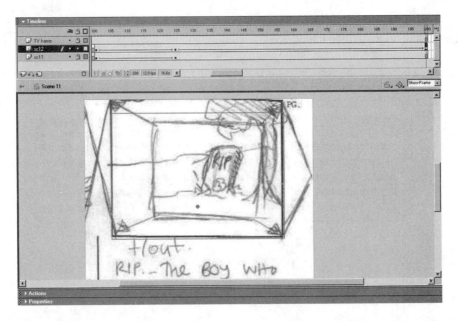

Finally, add the fade to black, insert a new layer, and keyframe on frame 150, then copy the frames from Scene 5 or 8 then paste them to sc11 as we did before.

You'll notice that Flash will add extra frames to the tail of the scene past the 200 mark in the new layer; you can delete these frames by highlighting them and selecting Insert > Remove Frames or SHIFT + F5.

So the end of your timeline should look like this:

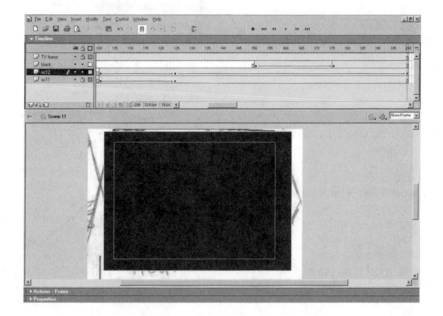

Since we have combined Scene 12 with Scene 11 (as layers sc11 and sc12), we will now want to delete Scene 12 from the movie. To do this go to Scene 12, then select Insert > Remove Scene.

You will then be asked of you want to Permanently delete "Scene 12"? Click OK.

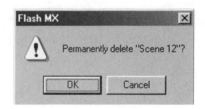

Take a peek

With all our scenes in place and camera moves set up, our first cut of the animatic is done. You can go ahead and preview it now (that's Control > Test Movie or CTRL/⌘ + ENTER).

In the next chapter, we'll import and add the sound, in our case dialogue, and then refine the timing of our animatic.

Over to you

Now you need to take the storyboard that you have created for your own project and import it into Flash to create an animatic. This will allow you to get a feel for your film and start you thinking about timing.

- First, set your movie properties: the frame rate and the aspect ratio.

- Think about whether your movie is destined just for the Internet or if it will be shown on video, in which case you will need to set the TV cut off.

- Import your storyboard into Flash, scale the panels, and then add or delete frames as necessary to adjust the timing of your movie.

- Now you need to create each individual scene of your movie and import the appropriate storyboard panels into each one. At this stage you can start to manipulate your images in Flash by converting them to symbols and adding basic tweens.

- Start to insert basic camera moves, such as pans, trucks, and fades.

Take a look at `animatic all scenes.fla`, (available for download at the friends of Ed web site), for guidance. You should see your film really coming together now, but the fun is just beginning, we'll now turn our attention to importing sound.

6: Layout 2—SOUND & TESTING

Sound is an integral part of any film and has been since films were referred to as 'talkies', as opposed to 'silents'. Dialogue, especially, connects the audience to the characters. What they say defines who they are and furthers the narrative. You've now got a very basic animatic in Flash. In this chapter, we'll be importing and adding sound effects and dialogue, and using this to polish the timing of our film a little further.

It's said that an audience will put up with grainy footage and poor visuals in a movie, but bad sound will alienate them almost immediately. This is probably true to some degree. In our world, a world of home PCs and $20 condenser microphones, practical necessities dictate the level to which we can aspire. Having said that, fairly decent sound quality is attainable.

Recording and importing sound

What we'll now look at is recording, importing and placing dialogue into the appropriate scenes in our film. Doing this at an early stage will help us to get a better feel for the pace of the movie when we start testing the animatic, and also make timing changes before we start animation.

There are many different third party sound programs you can use to record your voices, and which one you choose is entirely up to you. A good one is Cool Edit 2000, and a trial version is available over the net (at www.syntrillium.com/download). Cool Edit 2000 contains all the tools you'll need, but you may find that there's already a basic sound recording and editing package installed on your system.

File types and quality

Flash can import a variety of different sound file types including WAV, AIFF and MP3 files, which tend to be the most common. Which type you use will depend mostly on your type of computer, for PC users – WAV files, and for MAC users – AIFF files.

The next thing to consider is the quality of your sound. Although higher quality sounds will obviously sound better they can increase the size of your movie and affect the way it streams over the net.

Flash offers a variety of different sound settings when publishing your movie, and it's always best to import your sounds at the highest quality available then reduce the quality settings when you publish your movie. No matter what output setting you choose, if your sound has been imported at low quality, then that is going to be the maximum output quality you can get.

Sounds recorded at CD quality (44khz and 16 bit) are best. However, if you're recording your dialogue yourself, then the final quality of your sound will depend on the type of equipment you have – your microphone, soundcard, and even the room you record in, will all determine the final sound quality. Experimenting is the best, and most fun way to get sound that you're happy with, and we'll have to leave that up to you.

Obviously, if you're making a professional production, then you'll need to have your recordings done at a professional sound studio. For most cartoons made for the Internet, with a little trial and error you should be able to get recordings that will satisfy you and that are good enough to publish with most standard home computing equipment.

Editing

After you've recorded your sound, one important thing to do is edit your sound files into individual lines of dialogue. When recording dialogue it's most easy to record an entire sequence, but when it comes to animating to it, especially if there are different lines that are spread out over different scenes, it's much easier to have them broken down into smaller and separate files. It is possible to do this editing in Flash, but with experience, it proves easier to have done it before you import your files.

Of course there are plenty of things you can do to your sound once it's on your computer, as well as plenty of ways to have obtained the noise or effects that your cartoon needs. It really is up to you. One quick piece of advice though, is to save each line of dialogue or sound effect with a filename that tells you exactly what it is. Unlike pictures, there isn't any quick way of previewing, and you'll kick yourself if you have to listen to each and every sound whenever you need to find a particular line or effect.

Importing

Once you've got all your dialogue recorded and saved as the appropriate file types, it,s time to import it into Flash. Since our first line of dialog appears in Scene 2, let's start there.

Available for download (from www.friendsofED.com) are all the WAV files that we've used in 'The Boy Who Cried Wolf', if you've not got the time right now to record your own files.

Go to File > Import, just as we did when we imported our storyboard images and an Import dialog box will appear.

Depending on the type of files you're going to import, some may not be visible. If this is the case, select Files of type: All Files (*.*).

It's easiest to import all of your sound files at the same time. You can do this by selecting the first file and then holding down the SHIFT key as you select the others. Click Open. Flash will now place all of the sound files in your Library.

Before we can bring the sounds into the scene, we must create a layer for them. Create a new layer in the scene below the storyboard layer and label it 'dialogue'.

In our dialogue layer, we need to create a keyframe for where we want this line of dialogue to commence. At this point it's not really that important as we'll make adjustments in the next step.

On frame 5 of the scene, insert a new keyframe and make sure that it's selected. Then from your Library select the line of dialogue, in this case wolf 01.

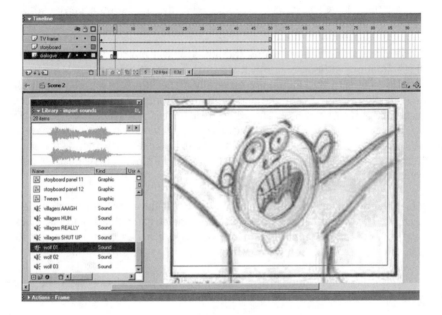

While holding down the left mouse button, drag it out onto the stage. Flash will now have placed the sound in the timeline starting at frame five. You'll be able to see it graphically represented as a sound waveform.

We've now added our first line of dialogue to our animatic.

Playing sound in Flash

Before we go any further, let's take a look at the way Flash plays sound. There are two options for playing sound in Flash – **event** sounds and **streaming** sounds. They differ mostly in the way that they're triggered, but there are a number of things that will affect your decision to use one method over the other.

Event sounds

When you select this option, Flash is basically playing the sound in much the same way it plays a symbol. It will load one version of the sound and re-use it every time the sound is played. This is good for sound effects and sounds that you intend to re-use.

There are problems with this type of sound though, as it will not always sync up with (play properly or alongside) the animation. Although Flash will start the sound at the correct place in the timeline, it will not always play in sync with the animation, especially if the film is being played on a slower computer. This is because Flash is playing the sound and animation independently from each other. It will load the entire sound before it starts playing it and when it does, it is not synced to the timeline, except for its start position. Therefore, if Flash is loading and playing the animation frame-by-frame, and it slows down (because the computer takes longer to load the frames than to play them), the sound will eventually become out of sync with the animation. This is a problem with dialogue especially, because we want the mouth movements to match to the sound exactly.

Another problem with using event sounds is that Flash must have the sound completely loaded before it can start playing it. This will affect the way your animation streams (loads and plays over the Internet) as Flash will have to wait for the entire sound to load before it can continue to play the animation. It's therefore best to only use event sounds for short sounds that are small in file size.

Another issue with using event sounds for animation is, that you can only hear the sound when you test or publish your movie – this becomes important when we're animating to dialogue.

There will be more on when to use event sounds (and how best to avoid problems with them) in the Flash Animation chapter.

Streaming sounds

When you select this option, Flash basically breaks the sound down frame-by-frame and sends it out one frame at a time with the animation, meaning that it is directly linked to the timeline over each frame. This keeps the animation in sync with the sound.

However, as Flash has to load the sound one frame at a time, as well as the animation, this can also cause problems. If things start to lag (especially on older computers or across slow Internet connections), Flash will either stop the animation until the next part of the sound is loaded, or skip frames of animation in order to keep up with the sound.

There are ways to help avoid this when publishing your movie we will discuss them in the outputting and publishing chapter.

> *There is also a problem with streaming sounds when it comes to stereo tracks. When Flash publishes a streaming sound, it will mix down any stereo tracks into a single channel mono track. So if you need a sound in stereo, it must be played in Flash as an event sound.*

Another thing to consider when using streaming sounds is, since Flash does not keep a copy of them in the computer's memory, it must completely reload the sound if it is to be used more than once. This will lead to a larger file size for the complete movie if the sounds are re-used.

In all, you will have to experiment with your movie at the animation stage with these two different sound playing options to decide which one is best for each sound. For the purposes of animating to dialogue however, we will be using our sound set as streaming.

Setting up sound within the animatic

In order to set a sound as streaming, select the sound in the timeline then expand the Property inspector and select Sync > Stream.

Flash should now have changed the sound to streaming. To test for this, you should be able to move along the timeline with the cursor and hear the sound.

Now we need to place the rest of the dialogue in the remaining scenes in the same way as we have in Scene 2, with a five frame head on each scene. Select each scene in turn, add a layer called 'dialogue', create a keyframe at the fifth frame, and drag the appropriate sound file onto the timeline.

Helpfully, we've saved each line of dialogue with a filename very similar to the text on our storyboard panels, so you shouldn't have any problems.

With Scene 11, we have two sound files. One of them is the boy saying "oh no" then screaming, so we need to set this up a little differently. First create a new layer, rename it 'dialogue', insert a keyframe on the 5th frame and add the "oh no".

As for the scream, we'll insert that just at the beginning of the truck out for now. You can either, insert a new keyframe on frame 50 of the same layer, and place the scream there, or create a second 'dialogue 2' layer and place it on frame 50 of its own layer.

Using the same layer, your timeline for this scene should look like this:

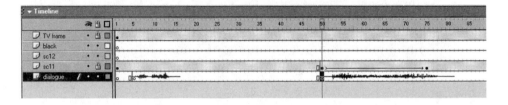

Once this is done, our animatic is now ready for our first sound test run. You should have been saving your movie as you went along, but now is a very important point to do a save. If, further along, you decide that you've made some huge mistake you can always come back to this version.

Testing your film

One of the great advantages of animating in Flash is that you have a version of your film you can watch at this very early stage of production. Building a film in this manner is very effective, especially when your film has to conform to a set time length. You can check the exact length of your film and control the pace and timing so that the key story points read clearly. Ensure that any action is cut for maximum effect and impact, as well as that dramatic or comedic moments have time to build to the climax or pay-off. All this can be achieved before any animation is done.

In traditional 2D animation this stage is called **slugging**, it is done with a stopwatch, with someone working out scene lengths based on the timing of imagined actions. Not nearly as effective or easy as our approach.

Let's quickly review what we've done so far. Our animatic at this stage should contain all our scenes in the correct order within the TV safe frame. All our basic camera moves are in place and the dialogue is inserted for each scene.

As we have stated throughout the layout process, everything has been set up so far with no real attention given to the timing of the movie. So as we watch this animatic for the first time it will probably appear to be very slow in places, and will give us no real indication of the final pace of the film. What it *will* be, is a very basic foundation for the film that we can now begin to adjust and refine.

So let's take a look! To test the movie, go to Control >Test Movie.

After you select Test Movie, Flash will load the movie into a new window and begin to play it. You'll find things easier if you Restore Down the new window by clicking the icon in the top right hand side of the movie window.

Your test movie window should now look like this and be framed correctly.

You can control the movie with the video recorder-like buttons within the Controller window. Open it with Windows > Toolbars > Controller .

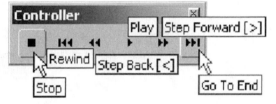

You can also use this to watch your scenes in Flash without using the test movie function. Like all the windows in the Flash MX interface, it can float free, or become part of the fixtures - we often affix it to the top of the timeline, but you'll be able to decide where it's most useful to you.

As you can see, our animatic is now cut together and plays all our scenes in order with our basic camera moves and dialogue. This will act as the foundation for our film and as the basic layout on which we can place our animation.

Testing scenes for timing

Let's examine each scene in 'The Boy Who Cried Wolf', and adjust them accordingly. In the same way we tested our entire film, it is also possible to test each scene.

Select Control > Test Scene. Flash will now load and play only the scene that we are in, the same way it played the entire movie.

Scene 1

As this is our establishing shot, we don't want to rush this scene. We need to allow time for the audience to read our titles and absorb the images presented to them. Don't forget, we're creating an environment and setting the tone for our audience.

If anything, this scene might actually be a bit fast right now, especially the pan. So to start with, let's slow down the pan a little. To do this, we just need to adjust the length.

We'll add another 25 frames to the pan. Select all the frames in the scene starting from the end of the pan (frame 100).

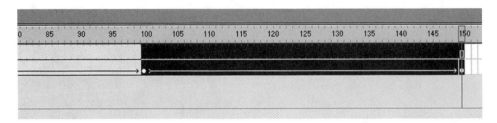

With all the frames selected, drag them across to frame 125. This will extend the pan and the entire scene, 25 frames.

You can now test the scene again to check the adjustment. We'll refine this again when we get into animation

Scene 2

We cut directly from Scene 1 to Scene 2, this is known as a 'hard cut' (as opposed to a cross-dissolve or a fade etc). The first position of Scene 2 will eventually need to match the final position of Scene 1 in what's known as a hook-up, but as we have not done this panel in our storyboard, we can just leave the five frame pause before the dialogue starts. That will do in place of a hook-up pose for now. We'll deal with this when we get to animation.

What we will do though is to make this scene shorter to end just as the dialogue does. To do this, select all the frames at the end of the scene from frame 25.

Next delete them with Insert > Remove Frames (SHIFT +F5) to leave the timeline for this scene looking like this:

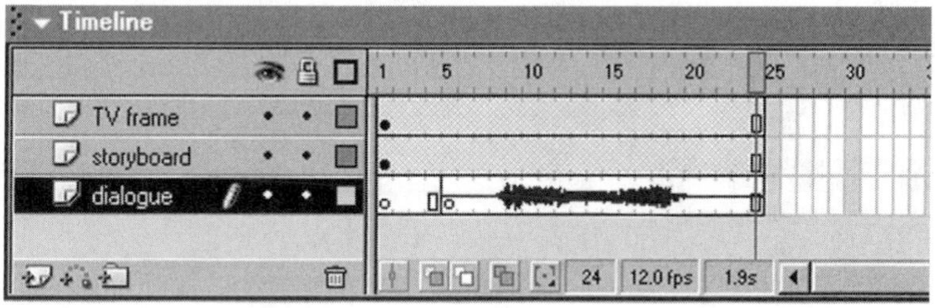

Scene 3

We will want this scene to start pretty quickly as the villagers panic, and end when the dialogue does. so let's move the dialogue to start at the beginning of the scene and delete the frames after it ends.

To do this, select the first frame of the sound on frame five of the dialogue layer and drag it to frame one. Then select the unwanted frames on all of the layers and delete them (SHIFT + F5).

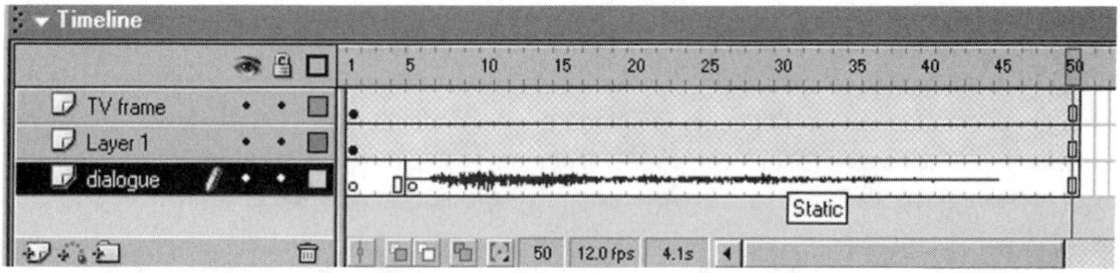

We've chosen to delete all the frames after frame 39, leaving our timeline looking like this:

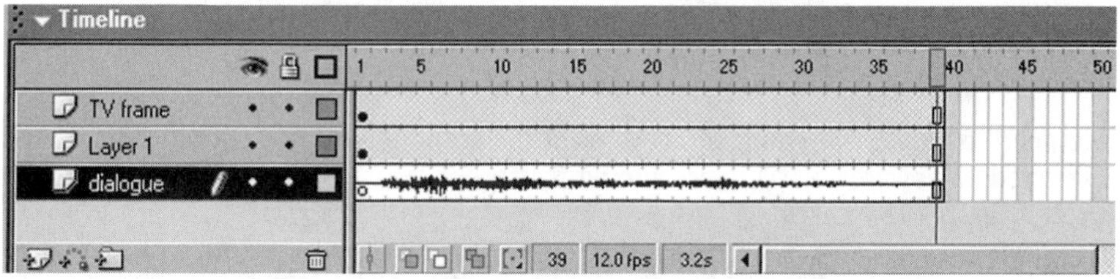

Scene 4

This scene holds too long after the boy's dialogue, so we'll cut it shorter. We want to keep the film moving and avoid dead screen time where nothing is happening or the story isn't being furthered.

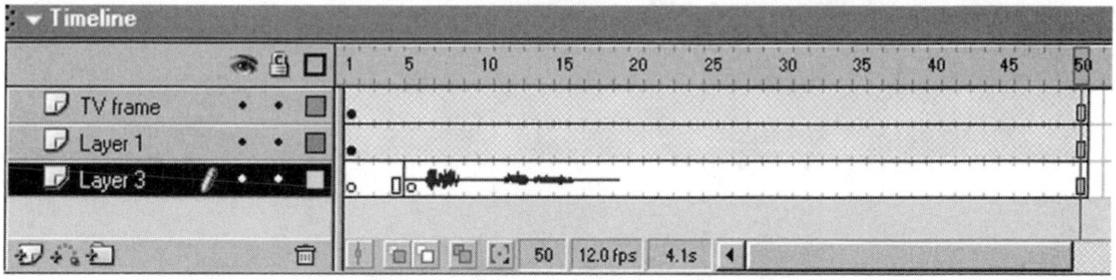

So select all frames on all layers from 25 to the end and delete them.

Scene 5

This scene is also too long for the same reason as the previous scene. We'll shorten it, and also shorten the fade a bit – again, for pace and 'feel'.

> *Like a lot of other areas in filmmaking, no hard and fast rules apply and personal taste does have a significant impact... that's why it's called art!*

To shorten the scene, we first start the fade earlier, so select the keyframe at frame 50 on the black layer and drag it back along its layer to start the end of the dialogue. We've chosen frame 27.

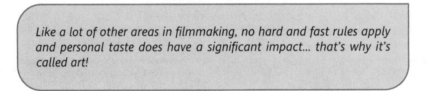

Then we need to delete everything after we want the scene to end, we chose frame 41 to be our last – so we selected 42 onwards on all layers and hit SHIFT + F5.

Scene 6

Again, let's shorten the scene to just after the dialogue, trimming off everything from frame 24 onwards.

Scene 7

We want to cut some of the frames after the dialogue has finished, but this time a cut right at that point would seem too harsh and rush the film needlessly. Leaving a few blank frames we've cut everything after frame 19.

Scene 8

Similarly, we're going to tighten up, and shorten both the fade out and the empty time after the dialogue has finished.

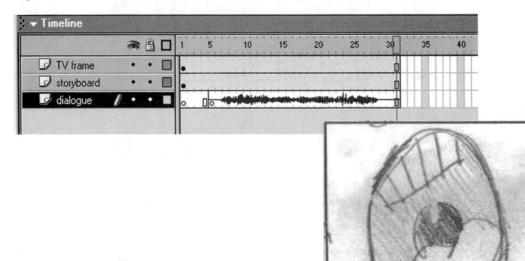

Select the first keyframe of the fade to black motion tween, and then drag it back to frame 20. This leaves us free to shorten the whole scene by deleting all frames after frame 35.

Scene 9

We're looking for a pace/scene length that will reflect what's happening on the stage, the boy's shouting "Wolf!" urgently – by removing quiet frames we're speeding up the film and making everything more urgent.

Scene 10

As the villagers respond angrily, we'll keep the pace up still by cutting the scene down so that frame 27 is the last:

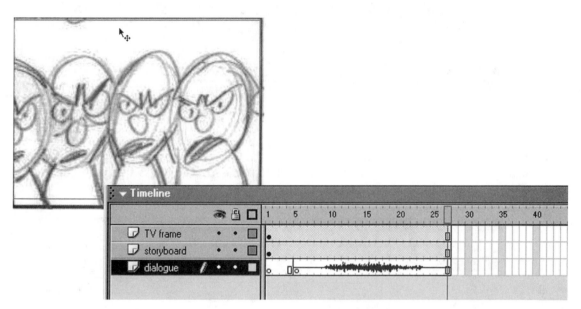

Scene 11

With all the previous scenes we've just cut them shorter to make the pace of the film faster and more dynamic. We will do much the same with this scene however, it's a little more involved, as its two scenes combined. On the sc11 layer, we start on the boy in trouble, then we pull back to reveal the wolf. We will want to speed up all this action to give it more impact.

Move the first line of dialogue back to frame three to start it quicker, just select its starting keyframe and then drag it along.

Then select all frames to the end of the scene starting at frame 50 (the start of the truckout) and drag them back to the end of the first line of dialogue, as we did with Scene 1:

Then shorten the length of the truckout. Select it's ending keyframe (frame 40 on layer sc11) and then click and drag it back to frame 25:

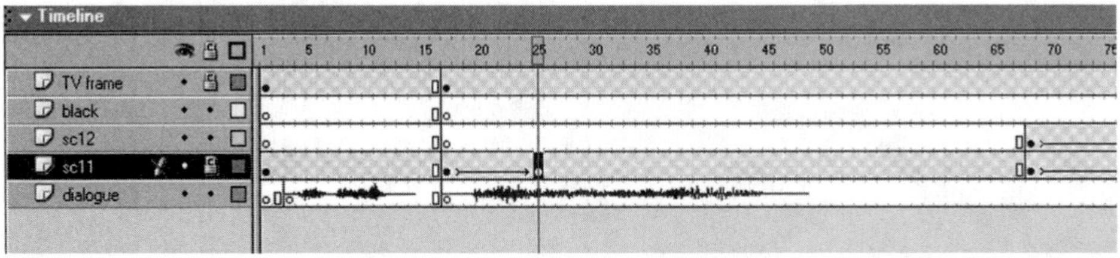

Next we need to move the rest of the scene starting at the beginning of the cross-dissolve up to frame 43, this will shorten sc11. We need to select every frame from 65 onwards on every layer apart from the dialogue layer, and then drag them along and back to frame 43, leaving this section of timeline looking like this:

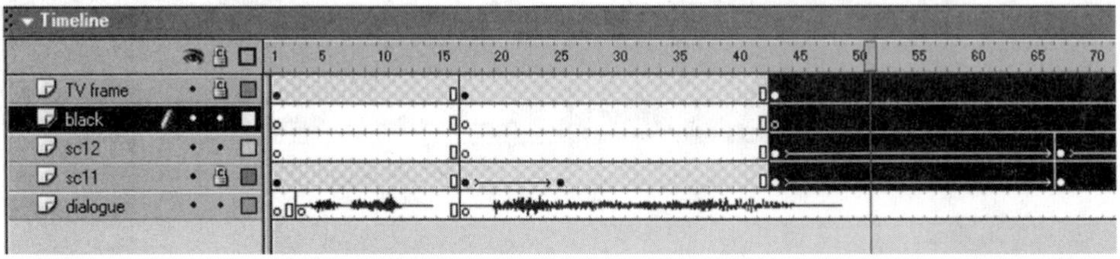

The second part of Scene 11 is actually another scene, sc12. We will also make this a bit quicker by shortening the length of the truck out and the fade. To do this, select the final frames of each layer and adjust them so the length of each camera move is shorter.

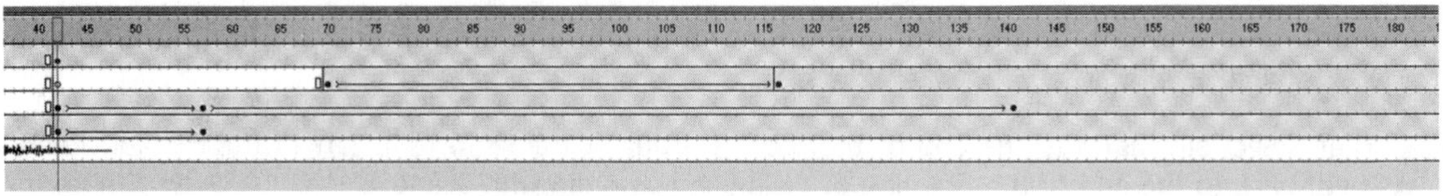

Then delete all the frames at the end of the scene from frame 116 onwards. The final timeline for this scene should look like this:

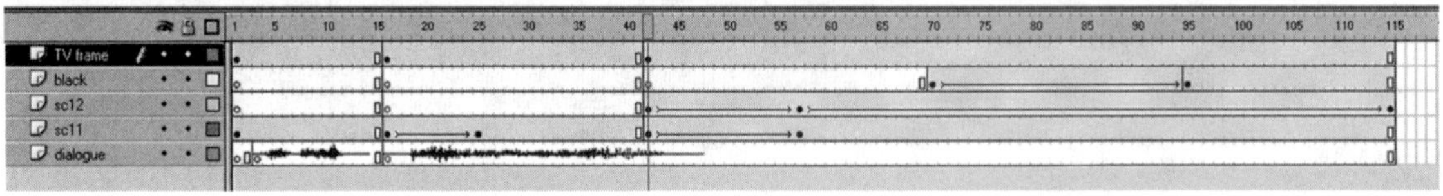

When we look at the film now we can see that is has become a lot more entertaining. Even at this early stage we get a sense of what the final film will look like and we can see how each of the scenes work together. We can also calculate what the entire length of the movie is and whether or not we need to adjust it to suit our requirements.

Over to you

By now you should have transformed your storyboard into a basic animatic. This is the first version of what the final movie will become. It is now time to add sound to your animatic and adjust its timing.

- Record the sound for your movie, if you don't have any sound software, then you can download trial versions of third party sound programs from the Internet.

- Edit your sound clips into smaller separate files and, name each file so that it represents the sound held on it. This will help you find the appropriate one more easily.

- Import your sound files into Flash and, decide whether they will be streaming or event sounds.

- Test the film in order to adjust the timing.

- Play your film back to yourself as often as you can. The more you watch it, the more likely subtle flaws will become evident.

- It's also a good idea to show your film to someone whose opinion you trust. It's surprising what you can miss. Being so close to the project, you sometimes can't see the wood for the trees. A fresh pair of eyes is invaluable!

What we now have is the basic structure of our film; an intimation of what is to follow. Your film has started to develop a character and life of its own. The next stage is to add the real meat of making a Flash cartoon - adding and animating the characters.

7: ANIMATION PRINCIPLES

So, you've got as far as making your animatic and you're ready to dive in and bring your animation to life. It is at this stage that many a good film has been ruined by low quality animation. So, in this chapter, we're going to give you a crash course in traditional animation principles, before transposing these techniques to Flash in the next chapter. This chapter is mainly theoretical, but it is important for you to have a good grasp of traditional animation methods, as these are the origins of the techniques that we use in Flash.

You don't need to be the greatest animator in the world to make an entertaining Flash film. You do, however, need a solid understanding of the basic principles of animation. Bad drawing and animation will alienate an audience as fast as bad acting in a live action film. If your idea is worth making into a film, it's worth doing it properly.

In order for your animations to be as professional as possible, we'll look at the background to many techniques used today to give you an understanding of timing our scenes and bringing a sense of reality to our characters though use of arcs, authentic weighting and timing.

Limited animation

Animation can be divided into two distinct categories: **limited animation** and **full animation**. Full animation usually involves drawing the entire character throughout the scene and has a heavy emphasis on realism. This style of animation is probably best exemplified by Walt Disney's feature films. The realism and attention to detail in these films is impressive, but this style of animation is time-consuming and expensive.

Limited animation can be seen to great effect in the old school Hanna Barbera classics. This method works by using as few drawings as possible to convey the story. Instead of redrawing an entire character in each new scene, the characters are divided into separate elements such as head, mouths, and eyes, so that only the necessary elements are redrawn. If a character is talking, we can redraw the separate mouth shapes and 'hold' the rest. This saves on time and labor and is just one of the many shortcuts used in limited animation to convey the story as economically as possible.

As you can imagine, with the constant need to keep Flash files sizes low (if your film has to get across the Internet), and the possibility of using symbols and tweens, Flash lends itself perfectly to limited animation, and it is this style that we will be focusing on.

Originally invented by television animators as a labor saving and cost cutting device, limited animation is currently enjoying a renaissance, due to the popularity of both Seventies retro nostalgia, and the emergence of Flash. As you are about to see limited animation does not mean that the quality of animation is any poorer, but it does mean that you need to be aware of all the tricks of the trade to successfully tell your story.

Key posing

The animator rarely draws every part of a scene. Instead he will draw the major drawings that describe the path of an action. These are the **key drawings**, or **keys**. This technique is called **pose-to-pose** animation, and applies to any animation, whether broad, physical action or subtle acting.

This illustrates a character standing. We've broken this action down into three major keys. The initial position is the character sitting on a chair. The second is the character starting to move through the motion of standing up. The final position is the character standing.

Notice that even in this simple example, the action of these three drawings may not describe the path you may have first thought of for a standing figure. Maybe you would presume the character would stand as shown:

While this example seems to make sense on paper, when filmed, it would look flat and weightless. Try standing up in this way – it may be possible, but it's not the way anyone would stand up, given the choice. It is important to always be thinking of the limitations of the physical world in order to create convincing animation.

Characters in the real world move in an organic way, very rarely moving any limb in a straight line. In animation, these are referred to as **arcs** and give your animation a more naturalistic and convincing look. This applies to even the broadest or tooniest animation.

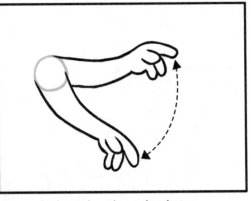

The path the animation takes between these two key drawings describes an arc.

Arcs can be easily achieved in Flash by noting where the rotational point of a limb is while you draw it, and then aligning your center point to this fulcrum. This makes rotational animation even easier.

The same rules apply to acting or more subtle movements. In this case, these three key drawings describe a head turn. You can experiment with degrees of subtlety. This will depend on what's happening in the scene or what the character is reacting to. Even in this simple example, you can see the arc of the movement.

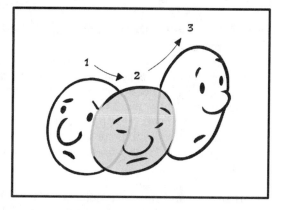

The key drawings are the main building blocks of the animation in any scene. Where we take the animation from here, depends largely on how far we're prepared to go in finessing it. In feature animation, this is barely the beginning. In limited animation, we would link these major keys in the simplest way possible, trying to arrive at a pose we can hold and possibly separate into different elements. Keep this approach in mind when animating in Flash.

Aim for arcs in your own animation, as this will make your animation appear smoother and more natural. When in doubt, try acting out movements yourself. In traditional animation studios, animators quite often shoot live action reference to help them understand a movement or action.

X-sheets

Exposure sheets, or **X-sheets** (also known as timing sheets, or dope sheets!), are used in traditional animation as a visual representation of time. They are the way the director, animator, technical director or animation checker records their ideas for the camera operator. In Flash we have the advantage of the timeline, which allows us to see the timing and progress of our animations, this is outstandingly useful for fine-tuning, but X-sheets are a wonderful tool for understanding your animation on paper without being constrained by the tools available on your machine.

X-sheets remain one of the best ways to keep track of artwork at a frame-by-frame level. On smaller projects you can easily use the Flash timeline, but should you be aiming to create anything complicated, then a good understanding of the X-sheet will be invaluable.

Film runs through the camera at 24 frames per second. So in traditional animation, we have 24 frames in which we can expose drawings. Most animation, even in feature films, is drawn on **doubles**. That is to say every drawing is exposed for two frames, or 12 drawings per second.

Single frame animation is used when a fast movement is required or there is a chance that the animation will strobe, such as through a camera move. Singles are also called for in other situations at the animator's discretion.

The X-sheet is divided into frames horizontally and vertically.

On the left of the page, marked Action, the director can make timing notes for the animator. These are an indication of how the director may feel the scene needs to be timed. These notes can range from very general suggestions to quite specific timing notes. It's quite common for this space to be left completely blank.

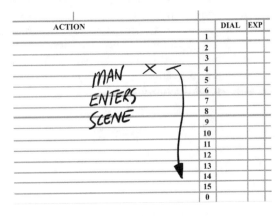

Then we have the frame numbers. Notice that the frames are divided into 16 frame blocks, this is a hangover from traditional studios, based on the actual number of frames in a foot length of film.

The next column is marked DIAL (an abbreviation of dialogue). Here, any dialogue is written down phonetically with any sound placed within the frame onto which it falls in the film. This lets the animator know where to put the appropriate mouth shape

In the middle of the page is where the animator charts his drawings. This is where the animator communicates to the cameraman how he wants his drawings exposed under the camera. This area is usually divided up into six to eight levels. These represent the different levels of animation – level 1 may be the background, level 2 may be the character's body, level 3 the head...etc.

The number of levels was limited to six to eight in the days when animation was drawn on cel and shot under a camera. Any more levels than that and the color would be affected by the amount of cell under the camera. With digital technology, worrying about the number of levels is redundant, but level order is still important, although six should really be enough in most instances.

The wide column on the right is for camera notes, such as the start and stop positions for trucks and pans, the field size and which background.

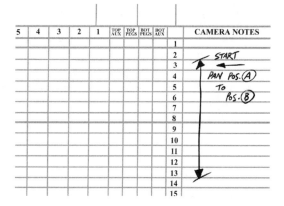

The rest of the columns in the X-sheet are thankfully redundant to us, the modern Flash animators, as they are concerned with the physical placement of drawings under a real camera.

In-betweening

You have probably heard of the animation term **'Tweening'**. Used frequently in Flash animation, this term comes from the traditional animation concept of **in-betweens**. In-betweens are the drawings in – between the animation keys. The animator, as well as drawing the main drawings (keys), also decides how many drawings are required between these keys to describe the path of the action and how fast or slow the action should be. Once the animator has done this, he passes his scene onto the in-betweener to flesh out the scene.

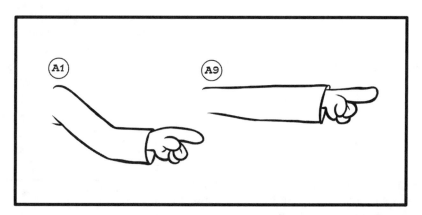

Here we have two key drawings. *A1* represents an arm, slightly bent. *A9* is the same arm, straightened out.

The numbering on these drawings corresponds to the frame number on the X-sheets: *A1* is on frame 1, and *A9* is on frame 9.

> As mentioned before, there are alternative systems used to X-sheet animation, for example, we could number every consecutive drawing *A1, A2, A3*, etc. The disadvantage here is that the drawing numbers don't correspond with the frame number. An advantage with the X-sheet system is that it allows you to go back in and insert single frame drawings.

To communicate to the in-betweener what he wants to happen between these two keys, the animator will draw a chart or grid on one of the keys.

This chart shows the in-betweener how many in-betweens to put between the two keys, and also how to place them. The in-betweener will first draw A5, which is half way between A1 and A9. Then A3 goes between A1 and A5. A7 then goes between A5 and A9. How the animator positions them will affect the speed or timing of the action.

If the animator decides to add some in-betweens timed on singles, in this case, A2 and A8, he would place them in the timing chart as shown.

Again, the numbering system we're using allows the animator the freedom to go in later and add these drawings without having to call them A7. Most animators tend to think in doubles, tweaking the timing later on, especially these days with line test machines being available to most professional animators. Flash also gives the animator the opportunity to view his animation as he's doing it.

In this case A3 is halfway between A1 and A9, so the in-betweener will draw this one first. Then A5, and finally A7. As you can see, in-between drawings are by no means always uniformly spaced. There are many ways to vary the position of the in-between drawings and this will affect the timing of an action.

In the example of a man standing up, we have three in-betweens between each animation key. Note the arc described by the in-betweens. In order for an in-betweener to follow such an arc, the animator would have to supply roughs. These are loose drawings done by the animator to indicate a path of action that is other than a straight line.

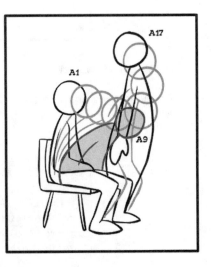

The timing charts for this action would be look like this.

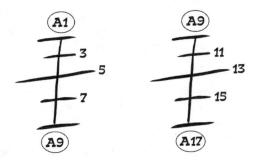

Timing

Timing is everything. Well, maybe not, but timing is a major factor in moving a character convincingly. The number of in-betweens we draw between each key determines the timing of an action. The more in-betweens you draw between two key drawings, the slower the movement will be. Where you place those in-betweens will also affect the speed of a move. Consider this simple movement:

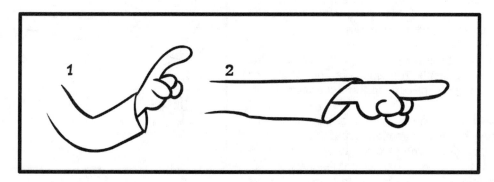

We have two keys, loosely describing a hand pointing. How we chart the in-betweens will determine how the action ultimately looks on the screen.

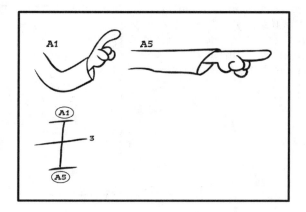

If we call the first key *A1* and the second *A5*, then there is one in-between (on doubles). So, we're left with a pretty fast action.

This is the same movement but with an extra in-between near the first key. This will have the effect of slowing out of the initial key and hitting the second key as fast as in the first example. This timing will give the hand more weight, and it will appear heavier. Unfortunately, it will also come to an abrupt halt. This timing will appear stilted and unnatural. The solution is to soften the stop.

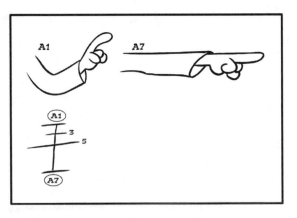

Cushions

Cushions play a fundamental role in animation. Cushions are how we describe the drawings we use to ease into a pose, so that the timing and movement appear more natural.

This timing will have the opposite effect to the previous example. The action pops out of the first key and slows (or cushions) into the second key.

Cushions are extremely important in making the timing of your animation pleasant to look at... nature doesn't come to an abrupt halt, so we need to always avoid abrupt endings in our animations, especially in limited animation, where the final pose may be held. There are a couple of solutions:

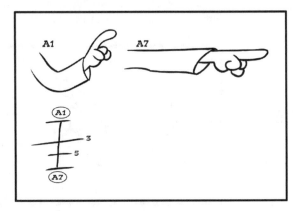

- The easiest way to cushion into a pose is to pop out of the first key and load the in-betweens up at the other end. You could time this action, in a similar way to the previous example, but with more cushion.

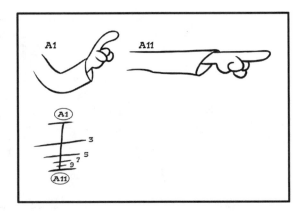

The extra in-betweens soften the move. Even though the distance between *A1* and *A3* is the same, the move would seem slower, or lacking as much punch.

- Another solution is to add another key. This gives us the opportunity to refine our timing. With two keys only, we're restricted in the timing options we have. Having an extra key allows us to have two separate timings for this singular action.

If we place one in-between on doubles between *A1* and *A5*, the move will be quite fast. With the extra key after *A5* we can cushion this fast action so that the point doesn't just slam to a stop.

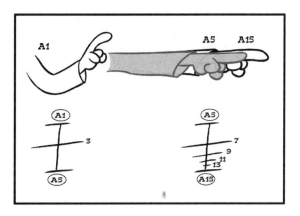

So, we can see the importance of cushioning in animation. Cushioning into a pose will give your animation a more natural look – even the tooniest animation needs weight and pacing. Apart from making animation look more natural, cushions allow the eye to catch up with what's just happened on screen. This is especially important in snappy, toony animation, where a character can pop from one pose to another. Without cushioning, fast actions will not read clearly and the movement will look confusing and unresolved. The audience will have a hard time following what is going on and may lose the thread of the story.

This action is of a character initially in a crouched position. He turns and straightens. We can describe this action with three major keys:

- The initial pose.

- The final pose.

- The cushion, which is basically the same pose pushed a little further, bringing the arms up.

We could time this action several ways, for example, *A1* with one in-between on doubles to *A5*, then cushion into *A15*. This will give you a fairly fast move initially, followed by the cushion over ten frames.

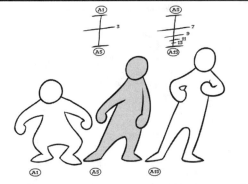

The use of cushions allows you to push the snappiness of your animation. Fast movements will read, because the audience has time to 'catch up' and register what has just happened. In this example, we've in-betweened the first two keys with just one drawing on singles, making it twice as fast as before. The cushion into the final key is timed the same way.

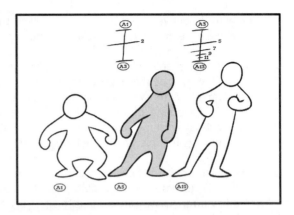

Using cushions to create snappiness

The last key drawing in a movement need not be the most extreme. In fact, if you want the timing of a gesture or move to be really snappy, then the most extreme key should be the one before the last. You still cushion into the last key, but you cushion *back*. This timing is much stronger than what we've talked about previously. Examples of this kind of animation can be found in old Tex Avery and Warner Brothers cartoons. Ren and Stimpy also made great use of this strong, snappy timing.

The cushions used in Ren and Stimpy were very tightly controlled. The number of in-betweens used in the cushions was kept down to one or two. The result is that the movement is not softened, in the same way that it would have been if three or four in-betweens had been used as cushioning.

Let's look at the timing of this point:

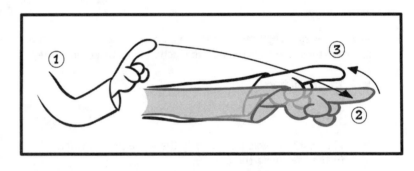

In the move from the first key to the second, we could get away with no in-betweens at all. Or we could put one on singles; this would not only smooth out the action, but also give us the chance to tweak the timing, even between this broad, simple move:

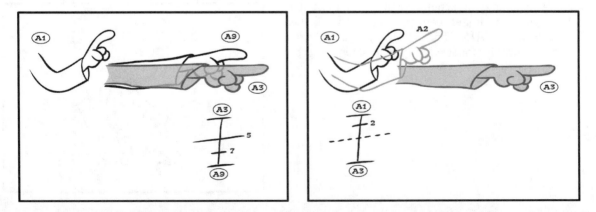

The dotted line represents the halfway point. This is where the in-between would normally place a kind of default setting. Often, especially in feature animation, the animator will draw a chart like this for the in-betweener to follow. This adds subtlety to the timing as well as really messing with the in-betweener's head. In this example, placing the in-between close to the first key could help the point read without losing the "punch". It hasn't altered the timing as the in-between is on singles. Be aware of this option, even though it's probably more finessing than you'd bother with in Flash.

Staggers

Staggers are an animation effect that utilizes in-betweens and inventive X-sheeting. An animated stagger gives the impression of a character straining:

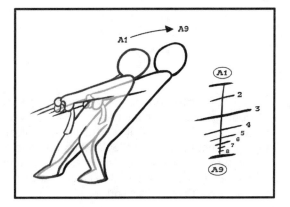

We've timed this chart on singles so that we can expose these drawings as a stagger.

Staggers work better on singles, so consider this chart. The effect we're after is a diminishing vibration, to imply a character straining and almost reaching breaking point. We can do it with this cushion by timing it like this:

The stagger takes advantage of the diminishing increments of the cushioning in-betweens, giving a completely different effect.

Another opportunity to use a stagger is when a character is extremely frightened:

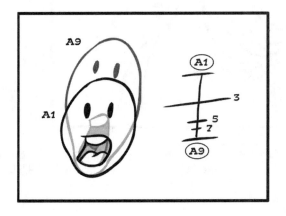

A character cushions up as he screams. You could time this as a stagger:

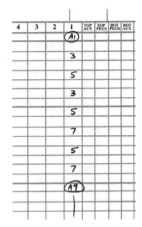

4	3	2	1	TOP AUX	TOP PEGS	BOT PEGS	BOT AUX
			(A1)				
			3				
			5				
			3				
			5				
			7				
			5				
			7				
			(A9)				

This is charted on doubles. Staggers will work on doubles, but they're a lot less subtle than when used on singles. In Flash, at 12 frames per second (the equivalent of exposing the drawings on doubles), they are surprisingly effective. The stagger adds intensity to the animation, making it a much stronger visual statement than the cushion.

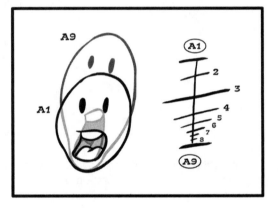

Charting the stagger on singles will make the movement more subtle, but also more intense. Expose these drawings the same as in the X-sheet shown above.

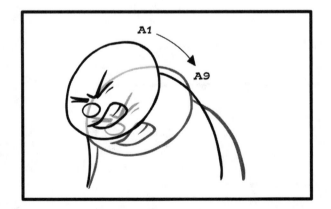

Here a character cringes, reacting to a scream or finger nails on a blackboard. The timing would be the same as the previous examples. The timing is generally the same: 1,2,3,2,3,4,3,4,5,4,5,6...etc. – two steps forward, one step back.

The common thread running through the use of staggers is that it shows the character under stress; whether straining, frightened or reacting to something horrible.

Stretch and squash

Even in the real world, anything moving through space operating under the constraints of the laws of gravity distorts to some extent, particularly anything organic (something to do with inertia and mass, apparently.)

This distortion is what we seize upon as animators to imply energy and weight; to make what we animate seem more dynamic and alive.

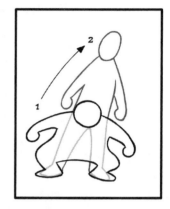

Here is an example of a simplified human shape demonstrating both squashed and stretched positions. To better illustrate the basic principles of stretch and squash, let's simplify these shapes even further:

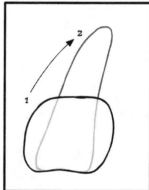

The most important thing to remember when stretching and squashing animation, is that the mass of the object stay roughly the same.

The principle of stretch and squash applies to any animated elements. In this case, the characters head stretches and squashes with the dialogue.

> *Of course, it's important for the character to look like the same person even when distorted, which is where the early attention to character design comes in handy!*

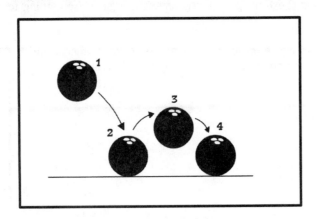

The degree to which you stretch or squash an object does vary. There are instances where you may not want to distort the shape of the object at all; for example, a bowling ball falling. Here you want a sense of heaviness and rigidity, even when hitting the ground and bouncing.

Weight

For a character to have a real sense of weight, the animator must primarily utilize the two previous topics: Timing, and Stretch and squash. The combination of these two major ingredients can give a two dimensional character a sense of operating in a real universe where the laws of gravity can exist, even if these laws are sometimes stretched or broken.

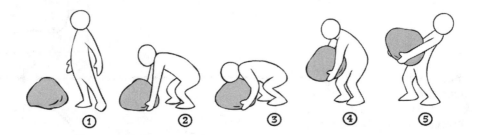

If an animated character had to lift a rock, he could do it like this. Like everything else in animation, there are several possibilities, but this is probably the most obvious.

Even before we consider the timing, let's look more closely at these key drawings and what helps communicate a sense of weight to the viewer.

Line of action

The line of action is a line that runs through the character and describes, in the most elemental way, the attitude of that drawing. When an animator starts to rough out an action, he'll quite often draw the most basic squiggle to imply that action, so he can quickly move through several drawings, capturing the essence of the movement without any of the detail. To do any more than this would slow down the process and the animator could lose their train of thought. Sometimes animation requires the animator to 'get into the zone'; seeing the movie in his head and trying to get that action down on paper. He moves from one sheet of paper to another, sketching quickly, almost as if exposing the drawings under a camera and thinking of each individual drawing as part of a sequence; a passing frame in a filmed sequence.

The line of action on a two-legged character usually runs from a simple circle for the head through the spine and down to the feet.

In this series drawings, you can see the line of action change in drawing *1* to the opposite curve in drawings *2*, *3* and *4*. The line of action in these drawings describes the character bending over and dealing with the weight of the object as he lifts it. In the final drawing, he has lifted the rock and his line of action changes accordingly.

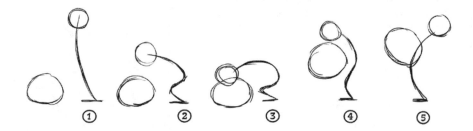

Such basic drawings, with just a line of action and maybe a character's head, manage to communicate a surprising amount of information, especially when shot.

> *Remember that often very simple things can communicate a great deal. This line of action example shows that the same action can be conveyed in a more interesting way, stylistically, with less work involved for the animator. Again, it really depends what type of animation you're trying to create.*

Here's an example of a line of action through a character hanging from a rope. The lesson is, don't waste time drawing if you're not sure the action is going to work. Again, drawings, like the film itself, are built.

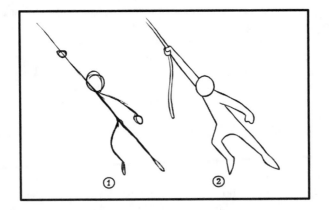

Weight isn't just about a character lifting weight. It's intrinsic to every kind of action or motion.

As three keys to describe a character jumping, this sequence of drawings would have no weight at all; there's no stretch and squash. The movement would seem flat and lifeless.

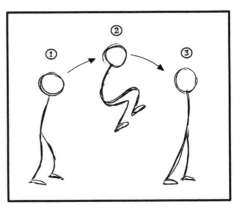

In this example, the character stretches and squashes, giving a greater sense of weight and realism. It's closer to how a human would actually move in the real world.

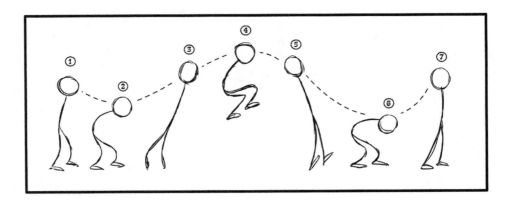

Even the most mundane action requires a sense of weight, not just the broader or more extreme actions. For example, a character walking:

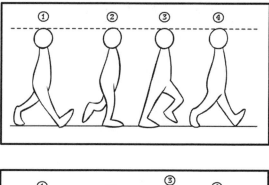

In this example of four keys from a simple walk, the character displays no sense of stretch and squash in his step. While the drawings on paper look like a character walking, they would give no sense of weight whatsoever. The walk would look flat and lifeless.

Here, the first key is the same. In the second key, as the character's weight comes down on his right leg, his leg squashes to describe that weight. In the third key, he pushes off with his right leg, stretching it out, giving a sense of energy being expended. The fourth key is the reverse of the first.

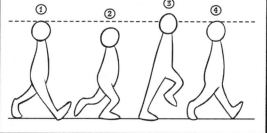

This walk would look a lot more dynamic than the previous example.

> *A word of caution – use the stretch and squash technique carefully, or your characters may begin to look like they're made out of rubber, which totally negates any effect of weight!*

We've primarily addressed weight here in the context of stretch and squash. We've used the drawings alone to convey a sense of weight and mass, and of being subject to a gravitational force. Where you place keys and in-betweens is something you can experiment with. One of the great advantages of Flash animation, as we'll see in the next chapters, is that the timing can be adjusted as you animate.

Arcs

We've already touched on arcs. Let's look at them in more detail. Animation can be broken down into keys and in-betweens. Where these are placed determines the path of the action. Let's look at a simple example:

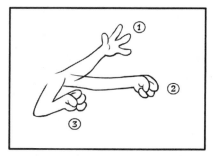

Imagine that these three keys show a hand grabbing something out of the air. The animator has already described an arc; in his mind, he sees the action following this arc, and may time the scene like this.

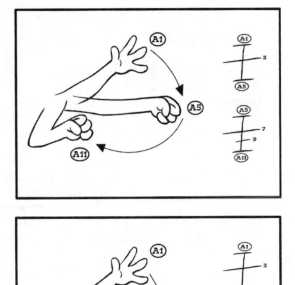

In a studio situation, the animator doesn't do his own in-betweening. An in-betweener's job is to place drawings between the keys following the animator's charts. The shortest distance between two points is a straight line, so a less experienced in-betweener may place the in-betweens like so:

These in-betweens will result in a disjointed and unnatural action.

Compare this to the movement described here, this is probably the most effective way to animate this action. It implies a strong sense of weight and motion. It describes a strong, circular, organic line of action.

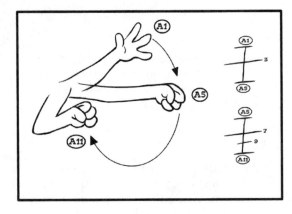

Walt Disney cartoons of the 1940s and 1950s really encapsulated the art of arcs in animation. Notice the great feeling of weight and natural elasticity in these films. The Disney animators more or less invented and refined animation as an art form, and by the 1940s, had taken it to a level unsurpassed, even today. The animated cartoons made by the studio at this time really are the benchmark.

Arcs are especially important to keep in mind when animating in Flash. Flash will most likely take the shortest path between two keys, when motion tweening to in-between an action, so be mindful of your arcs. You have to add information with either with more keyframes, or motion guides, but we'll guide you through this as we come to build our cartoon in Flash.

Foreshortening

Foreshortening is a technical drawing term that deals with problems of perception, when objects nearer the camera are made to appear larger than those further away. The result is to create an illusion of depth of field.

In this example of a simple gesture, foreshortening the right arm gives the sense of depth and three-dimensionality.

This similar pose, but with no foreshortening, seems a lot flatter and two-dimensional.

Admittedly, this is more of a drafting issue, but it is important to keep foreshortening in mind in your animations – in particular it will affect the line of your arc. Try to look into your drawings, seeing them as a rounded, three-dimensional representation. This is especially important in limited animation, where a pose may be held for some time.

Arcs, as much as anything else, will give your animation a feeling of weight and realism. The audience doesn't know anything about them, nor should they, but the natural, organic feeling of your animation is another pointer or guide post, leading your audience through the minefield of your film!

Action and anticipation

"For every action, there is an equal and opposite reaction". So said Sir Isaac Newton, and who are we to disagree? Theoretical physics may seem irrelevant to the light hearted world of cartoons, but if you consider the following scenario, you'll see where Sir Isaac's words come in handy in your animations.

A character is standing and then runs off screen:

Although these two keys do describe that action, even with in-betweens and the most meticulous timing, this animation would not only lack weight, it would lack any sense of reality whatsoever.

What's missing is a sense of anticipation. This is not only to let the audience know something is about to happen, but to keep Sir Isaac happy too!

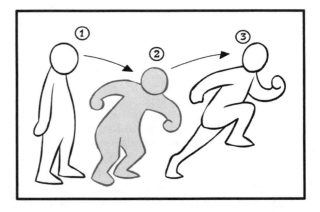

We start with the same key then the character leans into the action, squashing. This is the anticipation of the action to follow; the **antic**. The character then launches into the run.

This example of an antic is probably a little more subtle than most toony animation would use. We could go a little broader:

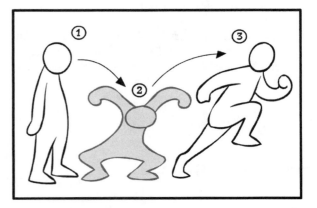

Here we have a much broader antic. This will make the animation stronger, but less realistic.

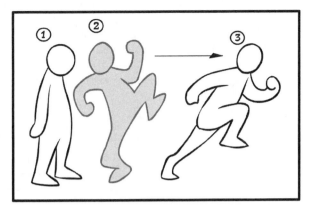

Another toony take on an antic into a run. You would probably cushion up into this antic with a couple of in-betweens.

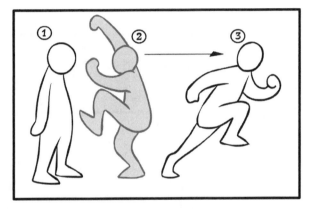

The zip off

This is the classic cartoon antic into a run or a zip off. A zip off is the great limited animation labor saving device. Instead of a character running across the page and off screen, the animator gets the character into the extreme antic illustrated above, and then, with the aid of a couple of frames of what used to be called 'dry-brush'... he disappears!

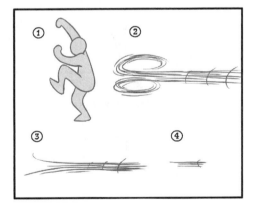

Dry-brush was so named because it quite literally required the painter to render the action with a dry brush, giving the effect of a blurred movement. You would have seen this effect many times in old cartoons. This effect was applied to many fast actions and was probably over-used and these days is seldom seen except in cartoons deliberately seeking a retro look or by animators who don't realize this smear technique actually slows an action down.

Anticipation is not only required for broad actions like the ones we've seen so far. The simplest or most subtle action requires some anticipation. To animate this point, the hand needs to come back into an anticipation before the final pose.

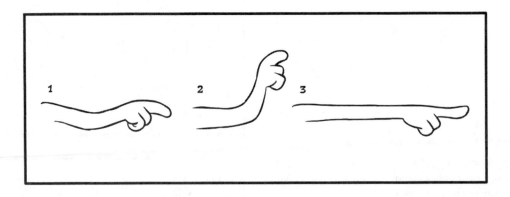

Here is a character going into a huge scream. Don't forget, the broadness or strength of the anticipation has to match that of the action. Here, the scream is very broad, so the antic has really been pushed.

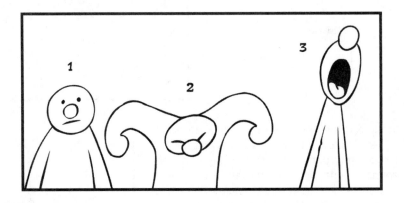

There are several ways to time this action. Here's one, incorporating a stagger:

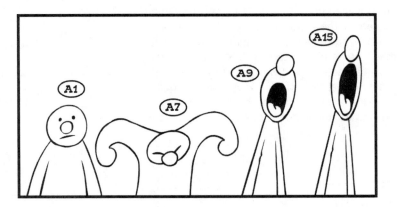

This kind of action is perfect for a stagger as the character is obviously under a lot of stress! For the stagger to work, we've added another key. We'd probably need another key no matter how we timed this action. We could time it like this:

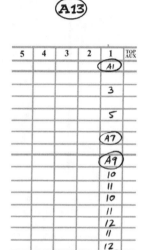

Two in-betweens, on doubles, cushioning into the antic (*A7*). We can then just pop into the action (*A9*). We could put in an in-between on singles, but for an action this broad with the approach we're taking (the cutting a few corners approach!), we don't need it. Three in-betweens, on singles, cushioning into the final key (*A13*), will give us the drawings we need to X-sheet a stagger.

We'd expose the drawings like this:

5	4	3	2	1	TOP AUX
				A1	
				3	
				5	
				A7	
				A9	
				10	
				11	
				10	
				11	
				12	
				11	
				12	
				A13	

The cartoon take

A take is when a character reacts to something, usually in an exaggerated way.

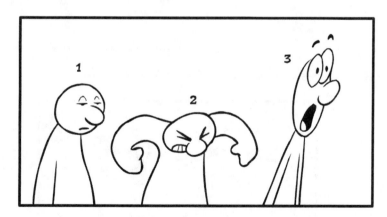

The take is a great example of anticipation and action. Takes are a cornerstone of animation humor. Warner Brothers and especially Tex Avery pushed cartoon takes to the extreme. More recent examples of great takes can be found in Ren and Stimpy cartoons. Every animation studio at some time or another has used them.

171

Secondary action or follow through

As well as the primary movements of a character through space, there may be parts of that character that develop a life of their own. These could be hair, clothing, ears etc.

This dog's ears are long and floppy. As the dog moves his head, the ends of the ears tend to lag behind as they are being dragged along by the action of the head; they are not instigating the movement.

If the same dog stops, then his ears will tend to keep moving, gradually coming to rest.

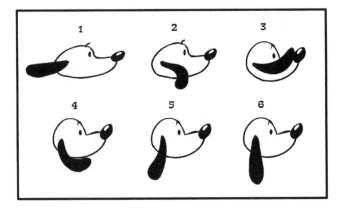

Any secondary action follows a definite path before coming to rest.

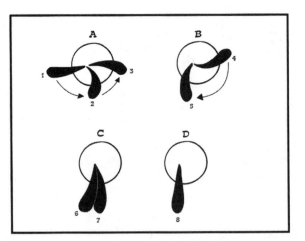

The speed at which the secondary action moves is largely determined by the speed at which the primary animation happened. This represents the speed the dog is traveling (*a*), as the dog slows down, the ears continue at the same speed until they reach their full length. They then start to come back following the path we've talked about.

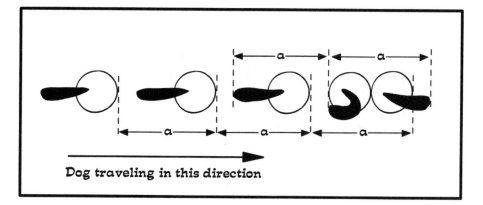

Be careful to ensure that secondary timing doesn't detract too much from what the primary action is trying to show.

Here a character comes up into shot quite quickly and then cushions into a stop.

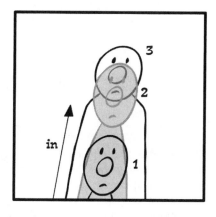

For the sake of clarity, let's look at the three keys like this:

If we put hair on this character and follow the rule we've just talked about, then the hair will follow a path something like this before settling into its final position. This looks completely over the top and distracts from the main business at hand, which is our hero coming up into shot.

A more appropriate course of action might be:

This gives the effect of a slight secondary action on the hair, without distracting from the main action. Secondary actions should enhance the animation, breaking up the timing so everything doesn't just come to a dead stop. It should never get in the way of what the scene is all about.

Action and anticipation are absolutely essential to convey weight and energy. The broadness or subtleness of the anticipation must always be reflected in the subsequent action. Just ask Isaac Newton.

Cycles

Cycles are a great labor saving device and pretty much a trademark of very early animation from early Disney to Betty Boop. These days cycles are often used to gain the retro look, for example, in The Simpsons. A cycle is an animation that can be looped to play through seamlessly. Most cycles are usually walks or runs, but any action that can be repeated, can be cycled, for example – a flag waving in the breeze, or a wheel turning. No matter what you cycle, it is imperative that the last drawing of the animation leads seamlessly back into the first.

This is a simple example of a cycle. This pendulum cycle works by merely X-sheeting the animation backwards and forwards. We've cushioned into both extremes.

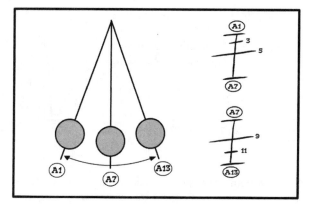

We'd X-sheet this action as follows:

To illustrate the more sophisticated use of cycles, where the last drawing leads into the first, we'll look at the most common form of cycles; walks and runs.

Walk cycles

Walk cycles are indispensable in limited animation. Think of the number of times you've seen cartoon characters walking for ages past the same repeating background. Here's how we do them.

These four key drawings illustrate the most basic walk cycle.

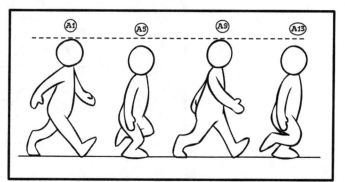

Let's time this example with one in-between on doubles between each key. *A13* will then lead back into *A1* with one in-between, *A15*.

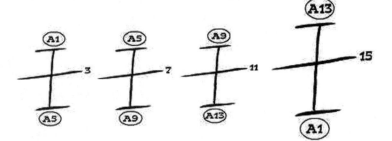

You would expose this walk cycle like this. This is an eight drawing walk cycle on doubles. You can repeat this cycle for as long as you like.

There are two basic ways to utilize walk or run cycles. Both can save you a lot of animation, as once the cycle is drawn you can cover any distance or time with these few drawings.

5	4	3	2	1	TPK
					A1
					3
					A5
					7
					A9
					11
					A13
					15
					A1
					3
					A5
					7
					A9
					11
					ETC

Here we have a locked shot – the camera is stationary. We want the character to walk through the scene. We hold on the background and pan our walk cycle through the scene at a uniform speed.

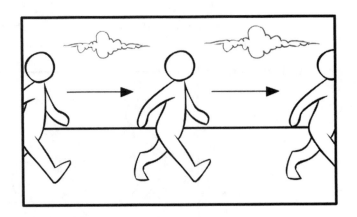

Here the character is center screen and the background pans through the shot. This is technically a dolly shot, where the camera, at least on a live action movie set, tracks along with the character. In live action, these characters often prefer to be called actors!

You can see from these two examples that cycles can save you a lot of drawing and are even more beneficial in the Flash context than in 2D animation. In the Flash animation section, we'll learn how to make a cycle into a symbol, giving the animator flexibility with walks and runs the 2D animator could only dream of.

An important point to remember when animating walk and run cycles is that whenever the feet are in contact with the ground, they must move at a uniform speed. If the feet don't move at a uniform speed, they will appear to slip against the background.

The best way to measure the speed at which the feet move is to mark where the heel falls. This way, you can control the distance the feet travel and make sure it stays uniform.

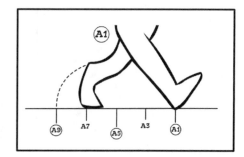

This spacing determines the pan speed; the distance the background or character moves for each drawing.

In Flash, you can create walk cycles using graphic symbols as we shall see in Chapter 8. A great time-saving way to do this is to make a graphic symbol of the character walking and then drag it onto your stage. If you then chose it to be treated as a graphic, then it will change as you cycle through your timeline's frames, allowing you to motion tween effectively so that the feet track with the ground in a realistic way. Once you're done you just change it back to being a treated as a graphic symbol, and you've saved yourself a lot of work.

When panning backgrounds in traditional animation, the pans are always executed on singles. This means your animation would need to be on singles as well, otherwise the animation will slip or strobe. Luckily in Flash, as we usually operate at 12 frames per second (Flash's default setting), the equivalent of timing everything on doubles shouldn't concern you.

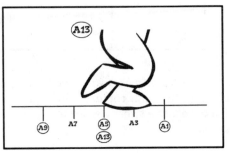

A9 is the reverse of *A1*.

A13 is the reverse of *A5*.

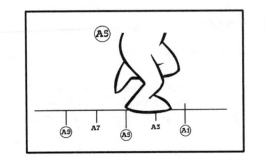

You can see how the in-betweens follow suit.

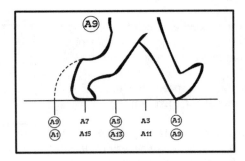

The walk we've dealt with so far works fine. But, guess what? There's a better one! The double bounce walk adds more weight, more squash and stretch. Nine out of ten professional animators prefer the double bounce walk!

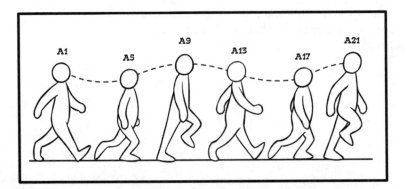

We would time this walk with one in-between on doubles. This is more commonly known as a twelve drawing walk cycle. The X-sheet would look like this:

As well as cycling a character through a shot or having the background panning while the character cycles on the spot, we can also have a character animate on a cycle to or away from camera. These cycles are exactly the same, just drawn from a different angle.

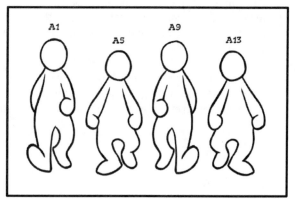

This is the same basic walk we've talked about previously. The same principles still apply; we've just turned everything towards camera. We would X-sheet this in exactly the same way. The double bounce walk towards camera. One in-between, on doubles, between each key. *A21, A23,* back to *A1.*

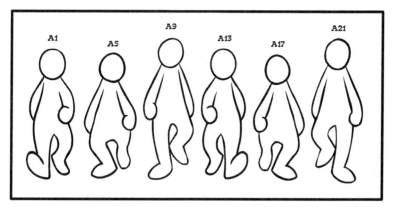

Expressing mood

There is a perception that animation can be separated into two basic groups: acting and action. The reality is that they are one and the same. The same rules apply: stretch, squash, antic, anticipation. Action can be effected by attitude as much as the expression on a character's face. Does a sad character walk the same way as an angry character? There's a bunch of animators out there who would argue vehemently that no, he doesn't! We say, yes, he does, more or less. One foot in front of the other, but it's all about how you draw them. Consider this:

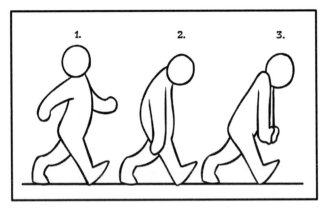

The same key drawing out of a walk cycle. The first – the happy go lucky generic attitude we've used so far. The second – the character seems sad or dejected, and the third – gives the impression of an aggressive character. If you apply these attitudes to the walk cycles we've talked about, they would convey the emotion required without having to change any of the animation.

You can, of course, refine walks to better evoke an attitude. Drag the feet, lift them barely enough to clear the ground, fiddle with the timing. This is a variation of the key drawing A9 from the twelve drawing walk cycle.

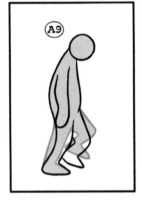

Here, we've kept his leg slightly bent, so it never completely straightens. His left leg barely clears the ground as it comes through. This will help give the impression of a sad or tired walk.

Swinging the arms through a shorter distance will also help tone down the walk.

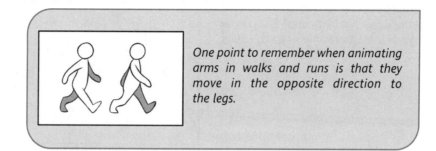

One point to remember when animating arms in walks and runs is that they move in the opposite direction to the legs.

When the left leg is forward, the left arm is back. This may seem obvious, but quite often it's what you take for granted that gets overlooked.

You'll probably find in the course of your animation, that you'll use a lot of walk cycles. Knowing how to animate them efficiently and knowing how to adapt them to a cycle, will save you time and effort as well as make your film look more professional.

Run cycles

Run cycles follow the same rules as walk cycles:

- Keep the feet moving at a constant speed when in contact with the ground.
- The arms swing opposite to the legs.
- We can cycle a running character center screen with a panning background or have him cycle through shot with a locked camera.
- Run cycles can save you a lot of work.

This is a fairly standard run cycle: A six drawing cycle, all keys, all on doubles.

Notice how much further forward the body is tilted than in the walk cycle. This implies a greater sense of speed, and the faster the character runs, the more we should lean him forward.

Comparing drawings *1, 2,* and *3,* we can see the character goes from *1,* a leisurely trot, to *2,* a run like the previous example, to *3,* a faster run. We can communicate all of this through the tilt on the body alone, without looking at the timing of the run at all.

The faster the run, the less the character should move up and down or bounce. In a very fast run cycle, there is really no up and down movement at all.

Drawing *1* implies a lot of up and down movement; a kind of bouncy trot, Drawing *2,* the run in our first example, has some bounce, but the energy is now more focused on the forward movement. Drawing *3* has virtually no bounce at all. A run implying this type of speed would probably have to be timed and keyed differently to the first two examples.

Here is an example of a fast run. This is a four drawing cycle, on doubles. We've drawn the character here with his arms outstretched. This implies a greater sense of urgency. When characters run really fast, the animator, especially in the Saturday morning context, would usually go for this option.

You could still swing his arms, but this can look distracting as the cycle is so fast. By a happy coincidence this is also easier to animate!

Walking and running is actually a kind of controlled falling. When we move forward, if we didn't bring our legs through at the appropriate time, then we'd fall over. When walking, the foot with the weight on it, is almost directly below the head. When running, the head is further forward. The faster the character moves, the further forward he tilts.

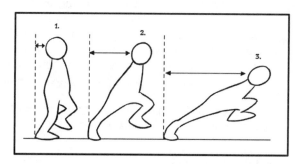

This is a twelve drawing run cycle to camera, on doubles. This run is quite slow and is more of a trot. You could also expose this cycle on singles to speed it up if required (the equivalent of a six drawing cycle).

Animating a run to camera is actually quite difficult to draw, as there is a lot of foreshortening. Care must be taken to imply arcs on the arms and legs, otherwise the action won't read properly. If a cycle doesn't animate smoothly, then any little aberration will seem like a hiccup as the cycle develops a rhythm as it repeats.

When animating characters walking or running towards camera, be mindful of where you place the feet relative to the body and head.

In drawing 1, the foot carrying the weight is almost directly under the body giving a sense of balance. In drawing 2, the character seems off balance. As mentioned before, walking is a kind of controlled falling, but controlled falling forwards. The guy in drawing 2 looks like he's had a few too many cocktails!

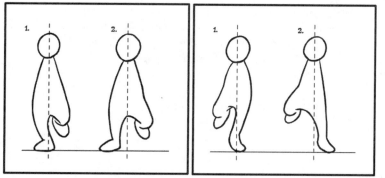

Runs are generally much broader than walks, so the feet can be placed wider than on a walk cycle. Even so, be careful where you place them. Like a lot of animation and drawing problems, it comes down to what looks right. A drawing should convey the feeling of the animation it's a part of.

Cycles can save the animator a lot of work, but it is very important that your cycles play smoothly. More than any other animation, the cycle has to read properly as the audience is going to see it more than once. Once you've animated a cycle, let it run on a loop until you're satisfied it works. Any annoying little tics will have to be ironed out. If it annoys you, then it will also annoy the audience, or at least distract them.

Walks and runs are a major part of any animated film and if handled properly can be a significant element in the make up of an animated character.

Separating levels

In the same way that we can separate mouths for animating dialogue, we can separate other animation elements to save the animator time and drawing.

We can break the design of this character down into separate levels:

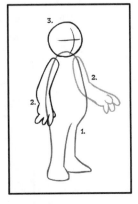

- The body, including the legs. We could separate the legs as well, but if he's in a stationary position talking and gesturing, then there's no need.

- The arms. We would have the arms on there own separate levels, one working under the body and one working on top.

- The head. This could be broken down into other separate levels; eyes and mouths.

We could separate the eyes and mouths in this way. Both on their own separate levels. In Flash, the eyes, for example, may have their own sub-levels (the pupils moving freely and separately for instance) – the principles are exactly the same though.

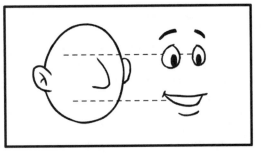

We usually separate the eyes so that we have the option to animate some eye blinks. The simplest way to do an eye blink is to draw two keys, one of the eyes open and one closed with one in-between on doubles.

We could assign each element a level on the X-sheet like this:

We've put the right arm on the top level in case we want it to animate over the face.

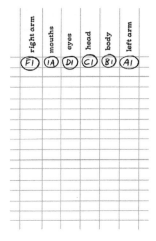

If an animation element is on a higher level than another, but needs to go behind or under that level, then you will have to register the animation.

Registering a drawing means that you cut the drawing off at exactly the place as the level below is drawn. In this case, we want the character to reach behind his back. As his hand and arm go behind his back, we'll need to register the drawing, giving the appearance of the hand working under the drawing of the body.

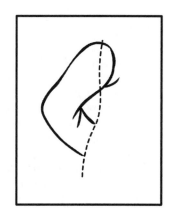

If an animation element X-sheeted under another needs to animate in front of that element, then we can swap levels as the animation occurs:

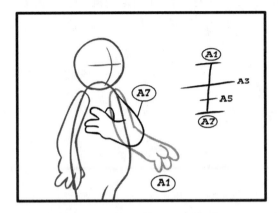

If the left arm needs to come in front of the character's body. We can swap the levels like this:

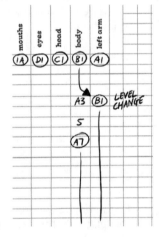

Separating levels allows the animator the freedom to time elements independently of each other. Mouths can be changed for dialogue, while an arm gestures and the rest of the character is held. You can have an occasional eye blink or animate the whole head, temporarily combining elements.

C1 is a head with separate eyes and mouth. C5 has all these elements combined on one level. C11, like C1 has separate eyes and mouth.

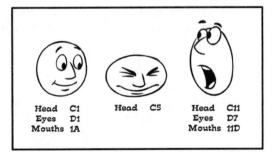

This method of separating and then recombining levels and elements is fundamental to limited animation and whether the elements are eyes and mouths or arms and legs, the approach is exactly the same.

Animating acting and dialogue

Acting is where we reveal to the audience who our characters are. Even in limited animation, the audience has to connect with the character on the screen if they are going to feel any sense of involvement with the story. The appropriate expression or gesture will tell more about what the character's saying than the actual mouth shapes.

Good acting in animation is very much the sum of its parts. Expression, eye direction, attitude, gesture, design and model should all work together to communicate to the audience the appropriate emotion. Here are some of the main points to consider when animating acting:

- Always make sure you understand the purpose of the scene you are about to animate. You have to know what is motivating the character to act in the way he does.

- Study the storyboard carefully to familiarize yourself with the overall story and your character's role within it.

- If there is dialogue, listen to it enough times that you can see the scene or action in your head.

- Make little thumbnail drawings to help you plan out the scene.

- Finally, *always* ensure that you have a pretty fair idea of what you're going to animate before you start.

Body language and gesture

Just as in the real world, body language in animation can convey a great deal to an audience.

Simplifying a character allows us to see how we can convey some sense of emotion without facial expression or arms. When you add those other elements, they should still work with a character whose body language and pose reflect the attitude evident in the dialogue and expression.

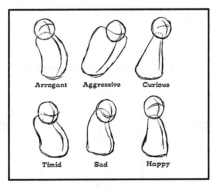

Adding arms to the previous drawings strengthen the attitude. This reinforces the attitude of the character, making it even more obvious to the audience how the character is feeling.

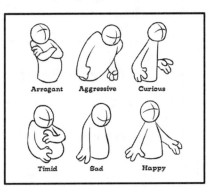

Facial expression

Facial expression can convey mood and emotion, not only by the expression on the face, but with the tilt of the head, both to the side or up or down.

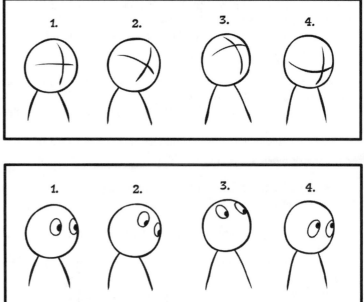

These different attitudes can be used to convey different moods. In full animation, the character may move through several of these different angles. In a more limited approach, you may pick one or two to convey an attitude.

With eyes, it further highlights the different attitudes. Even though the expression in the eyes never changes.

Facial expression is mainly conveyed through the eyes or by the relationship of the eyes to the mouth. The easiest way to show what kind of emotion the character is feeling is through the eyes.

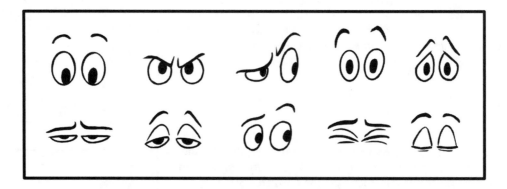

Make sure the eyes are looking at what they're supposed to be. If a character's eyes aren't focused, then it makes it harder for the audience to connect with what's happening on the screen. The audience will tend to look at the eyes first.

Eye direction is particularly important when two characters are talking to each other.

Panel 1 is a two shot. We've established where the two characters are in relation to each other. Character A is talking to character B. They are the same height.

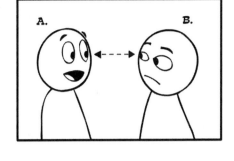

Panel 2 is a one shot of character A talking. He appears to be talking to a spot above B's head.

Cut to Panel 3 and B is looking over A's head. The characters are talking to each other but are not visually connected at all. The audience will also start to lose the connection.

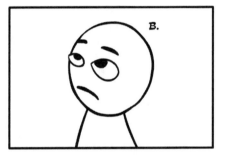

Characters don't have to make eye contact. Sometimes it's more appropriate for a character to be looking somewhere other than at the person he's addressing. Just be sure this eye direction has been decided on rather than happened randomly.

Looking away or upwards from a character can be used to imply consideration of an idea and therefore can be used for comic effect. People do this in real life – ask someone to remember a detail from the past and watch as their eyes flick up and to the side. If you ask someone about how something felt and they will most likely look away and downwards. Behavioral psychology is a very useful thing to have a little knowledge of when animating!

The eyes and the expressions they describe need to work in the context of what's happening to the face as a whole; eyes, eyebrows, mouth and to a lesser extent, the nose.

The facial features on drawing 1 seem totally disconnected. It's not only because they are so far apart, which doesn't help, but they seem not to be a part of a common expression. Drawings 2 and 3 seem more connected and cohesive. The position of the mouth in drawing 2 has an effect on the nose and eyes. The expression in the eyes on 2 and 3 reflects the attitude of the mouth. It's easier to read what the character is supposed to be thinking.

Dialogue

Animating dialogue is a lot more than just changing mouth shapes. Even in limited animation, you can choose a moment to accent the dialogue with some head movement, usually on the broadest accents.

The character says, "You what?!!!". Imagine a very broad read. He says "You", then antics through the "wh..." and stretches up into the "wh...*a*..t", then back to the initial head position on the end of "wh..a..*t*"

The X-sheet looks like this. The dialogue has been broken down frame-by-frame.

	DIAL	EXP	6
1	Y		(AI)
2	I		
3	O		3
4	U		
5			5
6			
7			A7
8	WH		
9			A9
10	A		
11			11
12			
13			13
14			
15			15
0			
1	T		(A19)
2			
3			
4			

> Note that the accents for the dialogue fall on the same frame as the sound or a frame before. When animating dialogue, even separate mouths always have the appropriate mouth shape on or a frame before the sound – never after, as the animation will seem to happen too late.

We'll mostly be dealing with the concept of separate mouths for animating dialogue. Occasionally accenting strong or broad dialogue can add another dimension to your animation.

Lip sync

In limited animation, realistic speech is simulated via a series of mouth poses, each pose representing a group of similar speech sounds. For example, the character with their lips together could represent an 'M', 'P', or 'B' sound. This results in a basic set of mouth poses, such as the one shown here with the poses labeled A through F.

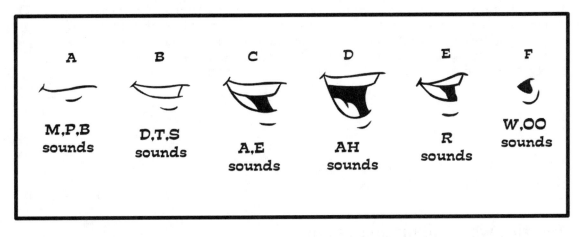

In-betweening them as shown will give you the B, C and E mouths. Beyond that, you can also add L and V mouths.

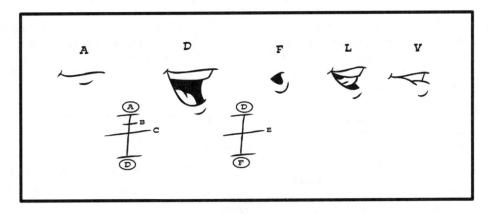

The A to F mouths can describe these sounds. L and V are named phonetically, and others can be added if you need a different shaped mouth for a particular sound.

This is how we would use these mouths to animate a line of dialogue. The character says: "I am very well."

> Again, note that the appropriate mouth is placed on or a frame before the sound.

Animating dialogue is no different than any other kind of animation. The same principles apply. In some ways, it's actually easier as you have a soundtrack that largely determines what you animate. Listen to the soundtrack over and over again, until you can see the animation in your head. Once you've X-sheeted your dialogue animation, play it back and see how it reads. You can then make any minor adjustments.

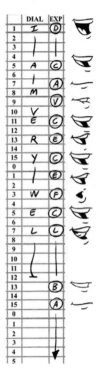

Top tips when animating acting

There are some things you should consider when you are 'acting' for your characters that are not really facts or rules, but you should be thinking of them all the time;

- **Less is more!** Twenty dodgy drawings are not better than one! A picture tells a thousand words, and a really good picture can cover you for a few hundred frames without anyone minding too. Don't think you have to have the characters arms flailing about for the sake of entertaining your audience. Most badly animated acting you see in films or on television is a result of over acting and gesturing rather than too little.

- **Avoid clichés.** These are without doubt the most overused gestures in animation. That is not to say don't use them. As animators who have worked on many cartoons, we're as guilty as anybody else of having used these gestures. If employed judiciously, then they're fine. There are animators that have used all of these gestures in one scene! Not a practice we endorse and nor should you.

- **Don't take things too literally.** Let the dialogue and the strength of your drawings convey the mood. The audience will understand what's going on without an over animated semaphore. Here is a very obvious example, but even on a more subtle level, animators can be guilty of interpreting acting moments too literally.

" I'm going...................over there"

- **Aim for realism.** The gestures you employ should be dictated by the scene you're animating – it is important that they reflect what the character's doing or saying. Try acting the scene out yourself. Watch yourself in the mirror and then thumbnail the gestures.

- **Avoid twinning.** Even if you do push the gesture for a more toony effect, they need to have some basis in reality. Watch out for **twinning**. Twinning is where the position of one arm is mirrored by the other arm, rather than being at least a little different. This is a common problem in animation and one that can give the character a stiff, unnatural look.

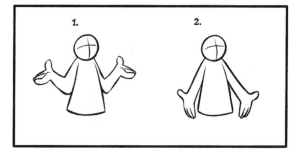

A better approach to these two gestures would be like this. Break up the pose a little so it feels more natural. Think about foreshortening and seeing your drawing as describing something in a three-dimensional world.

- **Think in 3-D.** Even if you are using standard symbols for limbs (a line with a figurative hand on the end for example) you can still put variation into them through the angle that they join the body at. Also, squashing your graphic can give the impression of depth. The viewer's eye is always trying to see in three-dimensions, you only have to give it the smallest bit of help to make it happen.

> *If the body language and gesture is right, then it makes the acting interpretation through facial features and dialogue that much easier.*

Working rough

In a traditional animation studio, the animator rarely does the final (clean) version of the animation. This is done by a clean-up artist, who refines the animators' drawings.

The reason the animator works rough is that it allows greater freedom to explore the animation without having to worry about refining the drawings. In our case, we're animator, assistant and clean up artist all rolled into one, but despite this, it is important to keep the two separate. Trying to work clean will restrict your animation.

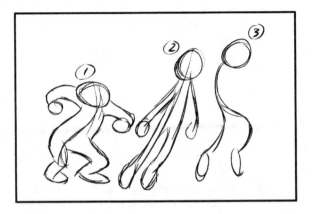

Animating an action requires fluidity and a sense of motion. These rough keys, while very loose are all the animator requires to get a sense of the action. Once the animator is happy with this movement, he can block them in, still rough, but with enough detail for the clean up artist to complete the process. We should try and work the same way. Draw your animations roughly (whether in Flash or on paper for scanning later) and then refine them when you're happy with all the action.

Using the model sheet

We've mentioned how to use the model sheet in the **Art Direction** chapter. These sheets provide a reference for how the character should look. Again, we don't have to worry about making our drawings look like someone else's, but we do have to make sure that our own drawings are consistent.

It's easy to go off-model, slightly changing the features of our characters as our film progresses, so refer often to your model sheet and when reviewing your work watch for model shifts.

The first version of the boy is on model and the second isn't. Sometimes, unless you look closely, the model differences aren't that easy to notice. Here they're obvious because we've got the off model drawing sitting next to the model. Characters have a tendency to morph; the eyes get further apart, the nose gets bigger. Before you know it, you're animating your character's second cousin! Be constantly vigilant!

Getting the feel right

Animation isn't rocket science, but neither is it as easy as you may think. The animator is the actor. His work is the human (or at least living) face of the film. It's what the audience primarily connects with. All the other important elements that go to make up an animated film are there to provide a platform for the animation to tell the story. You, the animator, manipulate the characters to tell the story and create empathy between these moving drawings and your audience.

Over to you

This chapter has provided a basic framework of traditional animation techniques. What you should be doing now is:

- Thinking about exactly what your film's characters will do that needs to be animated. Using your storyboard as a guide, make yourself more notes about each one, right down to the character's moods.

- Rough out the lines of action for each movement or gesture and use these to decide on key poses that you have to draw in detail.

- Decide which parts of the animation can be best achieved with limited animation and which simply *have* to be drawn in full.

- Work out each animated section in rough, but getting all the detail and information you can into the key poses and X-sheets.

In the next few chapters, we will take these techniques into Flash, so prepare to get your hands dirty again!

8: ANIMATING IN FLASH

You've now got a pretty good grounding of traditional animation techniques, with an understanding of how good timing and clever techniques work together to create realistic animations. The same principles apply to Flash animation as traditional animation, so let's get back to the computer. We're going to apply these principles to Flash to create some great animations.

As with traditional animation, Flash works by creating key poses and creates an illusion of fluid movement through the clever deployment of in-betweens. The key poses in our animation are held in **keyframes on the Flash timeline**, and the in-between actions are created by Flash, and known as **tweens.**

Motion tweening

In the Layout chapter we covered the basics of motion tweening and converting images to symbols, when we motion tweened some of our storyboard images to create our animatic. Let's now take a closer look at using tweens in Flash.

Let's create a quick example of a tween now – we'll start with a simple animation of a bouncing ball, as well as using tweens, we'll incorporate some of the techniques we covered in the Animation Principles chapter to make the action more realistic.

A ball falls to the ground and bounces back up. To make this more dynamic, we'll stretch the ball as it falls in, then squash it as it hits the ground, and stretch it again as it bounces back up, before regaining its original shape as it slows down before moving off screen, and out of our life.

We have made a rough sketch of this animation, which we will use to reference where to place our key poses.

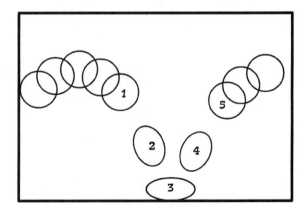

Open a new movie in Flash, and use the Oval tool to draw the ball, hold down the SHIFT key as you drag out the shape to make sure that it is a perfect circle.

With the circle selected, hit F8, or go to Insert > Convert to Symbol, and convert it to a graphic symbol. Make sure that your registration point is in the center of the image, as this will help us later, when rotating the circles. Do this by clicking the center square in the Registration grid,. You will then see it turn black.

In frame one, place the symbol in roughly the same place as our first bouncing ball key position.

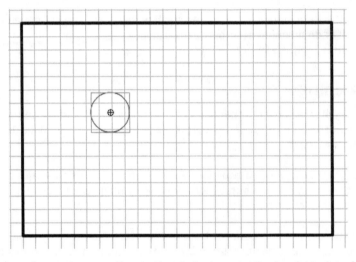

Create a new keyframe at frame three, and move the circle down to the lowest point of the bouncing ball sequence – position 3.

Notice how we have created a TV safe frame layer for this movie; this is good practice whenever we work in Flash to be aware of our cut off point, as discussed in the Layout *chapter.*

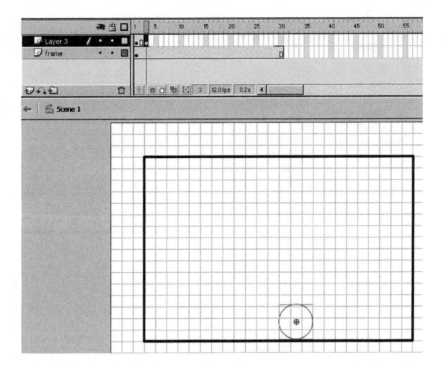

Finally, add a third keyframe at frame five, and place the ball in position five, towards the top of the bounce. Hit F5 to insert a new frame at frame 30.

Now click the **Onion Skin** button, at the bottom of the main timeline. This allows us to see frames before and after our current frame.

The Onion Skin function is the Flash equivalent of the **light box**, which is a drawing table that has a light under a glass top. Traditional animators would use this in order to see a number of drawings placed on top of each other, so that they could maintain the correct proportions and to ensure the drawings work in relation to each other.

The Onion Skin modes are located at the bottom left of your timeline. There are two different modes: **Onion Skin**, and **Onion Skin Outline**, which is just a variation on the standard Onion Skin mode, except that it allows you to look at the drawings as outlines.

When you click the Onion Skin button, you'll notice that a shaded area on either side of the red frame indicator, at the top of the timeline, will appear. This is to indicate how many frames will be visible on the stage. In our case, frames two to seven are visible. You can vary the number of frames that are visible by dragging the gray area wider or thinner.

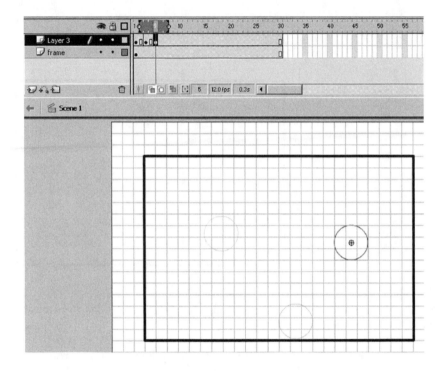

Now we want to distort the shape of the ball to reflect the action.

Animating stretch and squash

First, we'll squash the ball to the flat oval shape we saw in position three of the original sketch. Select keyframe three, and with the image highlighted, select the Free Transform tool from the Tools panel.

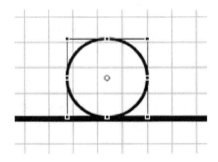

By grabbing any of the small squares that now surround the image and dragging them in different directions you can change the size and shape of the image. In other words, you can **stretch** or **squash** it.

Grab the small square in the middle of the left-hand side to elongate the circle, and then use the square at the top of the circle to flatten the shape. If the circle moves off the baseline, then simply move it back down again using the Arrow tool.

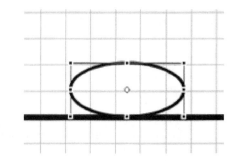

We now need to create motion tweens between the three positions – the easiest way to do this is to click on one of the frames between each keyframe, and open the Property inspector, if it is not already open. Select Motion from the Tween drop-down menu.

The result is quite close to our original sketch.

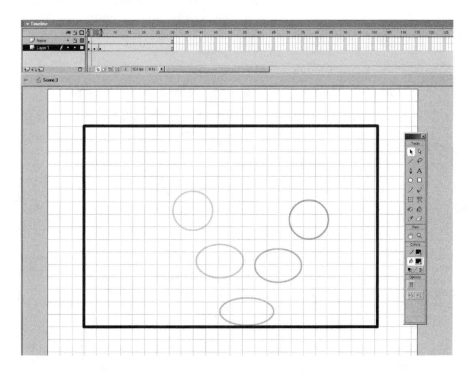

Converting tweens to keyframes

The main difference between these tweens and our original sketch is the angle at which the tweens are sitting. We can change this by rotating the circles at frames two and four, but only keyframes can be modified in this way, so before we can add our rotations, we will need to convert these frames to keyframes.

By converting our tweens to keyframes, we can also make our final film run more smoothly, as it takes less processing power to render a series of keyframes than it does to render a tween.

Select frame two in the timeline, and click F6 or go to Insert > Keyframe. Repeat this with frame four, and you will see the first two tweens transformed into keyframes.

We can now use another useful transformation function, the Rotate and Skew tool, to adjust the tweens to the angle we want.

Use the keyboard shortcut, Q to select the Free Transform tool, and then lock the tool onto Rotate and Skew by clicking on the icon in the Options section of the toolbar. This will prevent us from accidentally re-scaling the image.

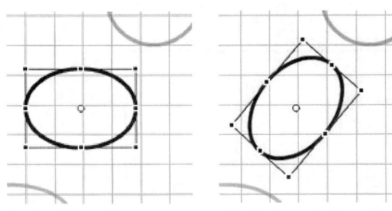

Simply grab one of the corner squares and rotate the image into position.

> *It is important that your circle rotates around its center point, which means that its **transformation point** (represented by a small circle) needs to be in the center. If it is not there now, then you can drag it into the center using the Arrow tool, and then perform your rotation.*

We have now animated the stretch and squash of the bouncing ball using just one symbol.

Now that we've seen how to stretch and squash our key poses and how to motion tween between two instances of a symbol that has been stretched or squashed, let's take a closer look at how to use this to create a more complex animation.

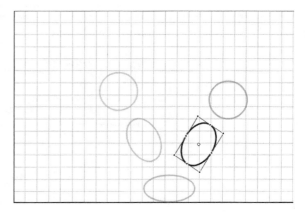

Key posing

Here we have the three key poses of a scene in which a character reacts to something off screen. Pose 1 is our first key pose, pose 2 is the anticipation pose (or antic) and the final pose, 3, shows our character's reaction.

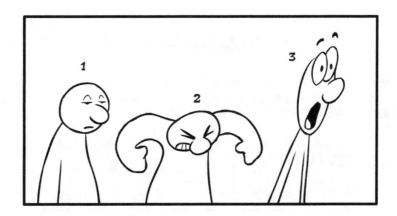

We're going to start our cartoon take animation by creating a cut off layer, as mentioned in the Layout chapter. This is not always necessary, but it is good practice to start each new Flash project in this way.

1. Create two new layers; call one 'rough', and the other 'cut off'. In the cut off layer use the Rectangle tool to create a TV safe border around your stage.

2. In the first keyframe of the rough layer, create a sketch of the pose. You can either do this by drawing straight into Flash, or download the file `Pose_One.gif` from the friends of ED web site (www.friendsofED.com), and go to File > Import to import it into Flash.

3. If you are using the imported GIFs you need to go to Modify > Trace Bitmap to convert them into vector graphics. This will enable you to use onion-skinning more easily.

4. We now need to create new keyframes for the next two poses in the action, so insert blank keyframes at frames five and ten (Insert > Blank Keyframe). Now draw or import the second pose, using the Onion Skin function to position the image correctly.

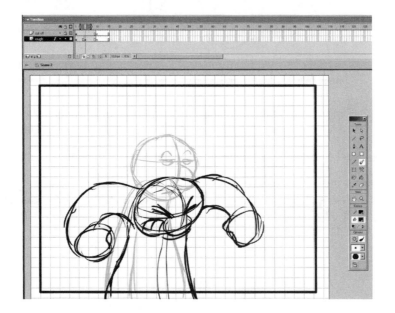

5. If you move across to frame 10, where we will draw the next pose, you'll see that pose 1 is no longer visible. To see all of the poses, you will need to adjust the shaded area next to the frame indicator to include all the drawings. To do this, grab the small circle at the end of this area and drag it back to frame one.

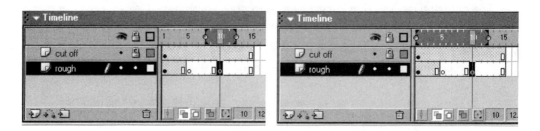

We can now draw the final pose while being able to see all of the preceding ones.

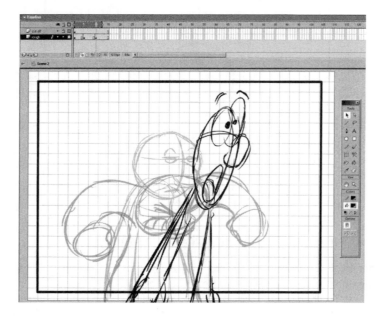

Cleaning up in Flash

Once the rough key poses are ready for each scene, the next stage is to clean them up and turn them into our finished drawings.

1. We want to create a new layer on top of our rough layer that we will do our clean ups on, and to create new key frames for the clean drawings.

205

2. We now need to adjust the layer properties. Lock down the rough layer and any other layers you have in the scene to make sure they are not accidentally edited. Then select the outline mode for the rough layer. This is the small square on the right of the lock symbol.

3. When you do this, you'll notice the drawing of the rough on the stage changes to a coloured outline of the image. You should now be able to draw your finished, clean, key pose over the top of this using whichever drawing method you prefer.

4. In this case we've used the Brush tool. You could also use the Line tool, or you could try copying your rough image and going to Modify > Smooth to clean up the image.

You can finish the rest of the key poses following the same procedure.

5. Flash automatically chooses outline colors for each layer; some of the light colors like yellow and pale blue are difficult to see. To change the color of a layer, double-click on the rectangle symbol for that layer and select a different color from the palette next to Outline Color in the Layer Properties pop-up window.

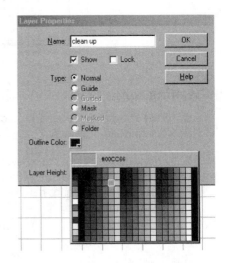

Remember if you want to hide a layer, just click the dot beneath the eye icon for the appropriate layer. If you are working with a lot of layers, then click the eye icon itself to hide them all and then individually reveal the layer you are interested in.

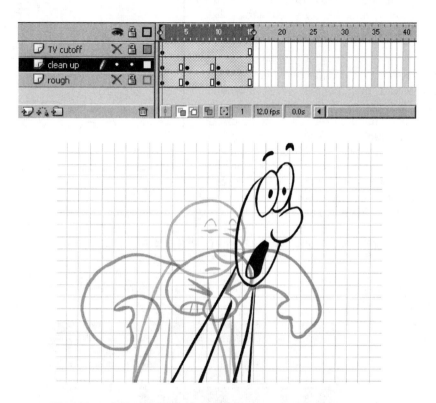

6. Once you've got all your clean ups done, delete the layer with the rough drawings by selecting it then using the trashcan icon.

> *Don't forget that if you get something wrong you can always use the undo function!*

7. Convert the cleaned up key poses to individual symbols, by selecting them and hitting F8. You are now ready to start animating.

Timing

These poses represent a classic stretch and squash: Pose 2 is a typical squash and pose 3 an archetypal stretch. We would time the scene something like this:

In traditional animation the in-betweener would create new drawings according to the timing grids. This scene would then contain seven individual drawings. In Flash, our aim is to keep the amount of drawings to a minimum by reusing as many of our drawings as possible – this helps to keep file size low. In our bouncing ball scene, for example, we used just one key for all of the action. In this example, we're going to take much the same approach by stretching and squashing some of our keys and then tweening between them.

If you look at the timing chart, you can see how we need one in-between between key pose one and two. We can modify the first key pose by squashing it down slightly.

1. Insert a new keyframe of pose one in frame four (just before pose two).

2. Hit Q to select the Free Transform tool, and squash this new keyframe into shape and position, just as we did with the bouncing ball. Again, use the Onion Skin function to help you position this correctly.

As this is the same image as pose one, just modified a little, this in-between will give the impression of moving slowly out of pose one into pose two. Maybe not as subtle as a fully drawn in-between, but it will work well, and it will keep the all-important file size down.

We now want to use **reverse timing**. In other words, moving quickly out of pose one and slowing into pose two.

3. Insert a new keyframe on pose two and squash it down slightly to give the impression of slowing into the anticipation.

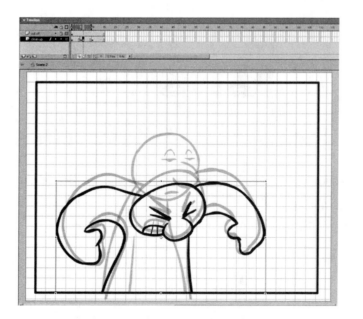

To move between poses two and three we require three in-betweens that slow up into the final pose. To avoid more hand drawn in-betweens, we can achieve a similar effect by taking pose three and modifying that for the cushion.

4. Modify pose three by using the Free Transform tool with the Rotate and Skew option. The image moves up at an angle, applying some rotation to the key can help get the image in the exact posi tion you need.

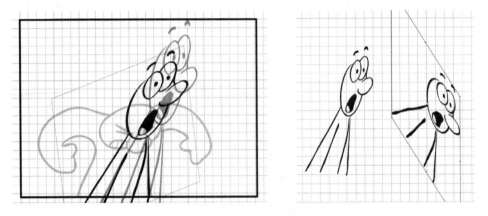

To apply this kind of distortion, select the image using the Arrow tool. Hit Q to select the Free Transform tool, and then click on the Rotate and Skew option in the Tools panel. Now grab one of the middle squares instead of the corners to reposition the image. You can drag the registration point of your image, to change the point around which the image rotates to create more realistic rotations.

5. Now, drag pose three back to frame seven, right after pose our modified pose two. Then insert new keyframe on frame 10 allowing for our two tweens. Add a default motion tween between frames seven and 10.

6. Now add another motion tween, again accepting all of the defaults, between frames one and five.

Here is our finished scene as viewed with the Onion Skin function.

Redefining and improvement

This scene is animated in the most basic way. We could make some small changes to our animation to add more realism. If you look closely at pose two, the anticipation, you'll notice that since it is one single drawing, the arms and head all move together, and in our first instance of the key, the arms are higher than the second instance that it moves into.

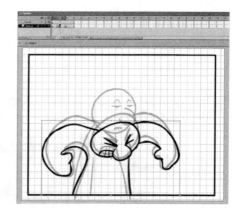

As this action happens quite fast, this would probably work fine. In reality however, the arms would move in the opposite direction; the head would move down and the arms would move up.

By separating this drawing into two elements, the head and the body, we can move them independently to get a more natural action.

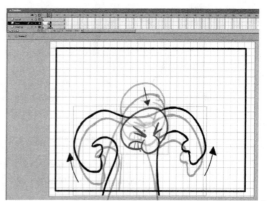

Doing this action this way requires no extra drawings, but you will have to cut and paste the head onto a different level. The results will look much better however, especially if it were a slow movement where we wanted to tween the two positions.

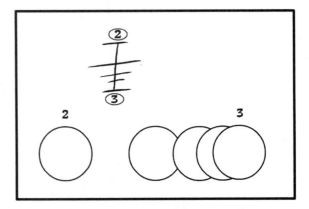

Easing

To cushion in or out of a key drawing in Flash, we can adjust the timing of the tweens by **easing in** or **easing out**. If we look at the second timing grid in our rolling ball example, we can see that the tweens between our antic and our final pose should decrease in distance as we get closer to the final pose – in other words, the action will slow (cushion) into a stop.

This demonstrates exactly what we mean: as the tweens approach the final position they get closer together, thus giving the impression of slowing down. In Flash, this kind of tweening is know as easing, and can be easily adjusted after a symbol has been motion tweened.

In this similar example, we have created our two keys and tweened them. Flash, by default, has tweened them evenly. Again, our aim is natural movement, so we do not want uniform tweens.

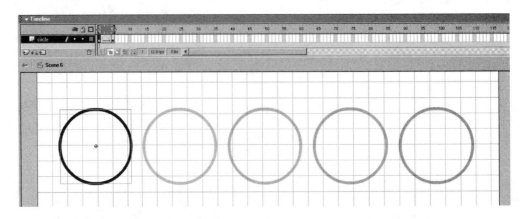

> *Remember, you can only motion tween symbols in your Library, and you can only motion tween one symbol on a layer at a time.*

To tell Flash to tween them differently, we need to adjust the easing. The Ease control is located in the Property inspector, below the Tween box. By using the slide control, you can adjust the way Flash times the tweens by either easing in or out.

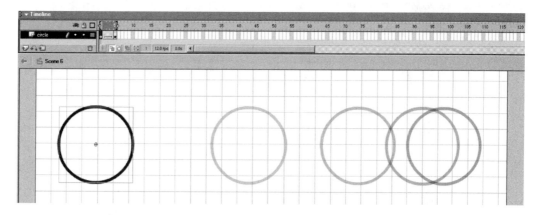

The Ease control ranges from -100 to 100. A value of 0 means that no easing has been applied to a tween.

Here's how the circle would look, first with Ease: set to 100 Out:

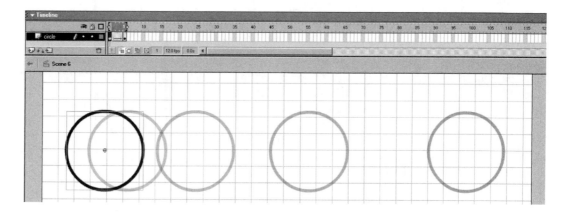

And with Ease: set to 100 In:

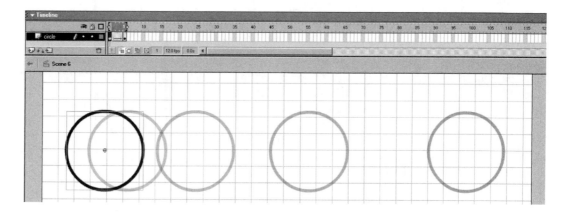

You can see by these two different settings how differently Flash may time your tweens. With this in mind we would therefore have applied 100 easing out to our final keys in the example of the cartoon take, slowing it to a stop.

Easing is an important function to understand. This function used within the principles of timing and cushions can add much nicer movement to your animation.

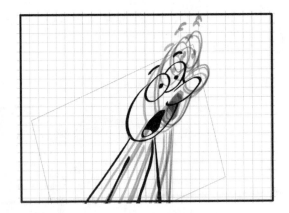

Pop and cushion

This approach to timing a scene will make the action a lot snappier. We would use the same key poses as the last example, only change the stretch and squash a little on the final keys.

In the image below, we can see how this part of the action cushions into the final pose – which is the most extreme pose. The term **pop and cushion** expresses exactly what this timing will do – pop into our most extreme key then cushion back to a less extreme key.

By separating elements, as we did with the anticipation, you can also add extra effect to this kind of timing. In this case, we've separated the eyes and mouth and stretched them separately.

Animation in Flash is similar to animation done any other way. It's a means to an end and that is to create entertaining and believable acting and action to give the audience characters they can relate to and have empathy with. The key to successful animation is to create this empathy and suspension of disbelief in as few drawings as possible.

A film is something you build and so is an animated scene. Test your work, watch it critically and fine-tune it until you are satisfied it conveys the message you wanted. The fine-tuning process itself can take many hours, even for a few short minutes of film – but it is an important part of creating good animation.

> *The animation is the star of your film. More than any other component, animation determines whether your film fails or succeeds. Give it the attention it deserves.*

Cycles

In the Animation Principles chapter, we saw how cycles can save much time and effort. So it is in Flash. They are also a great way to minimize file size by creating an animation and converting it to a symbol, and then using the symbol over and over.

Let's create a very basic cycle in Flash to understand the properties of cycles as symbols.

In this example, we have a rough drawing of a car and we're going to make the wheels spin in a cycle, we'll not only make the wheels spin, but we can also reuse the cycle for each of the wheels. You can download this picture of the car, `car.gif` at the friends of ED web site.

Symbols and layers

Let's clean up the car making two separate elements: the body and the back wheel. We'll create them as separate layers. With both levels drawn, select them and store them in the Library as symbols.

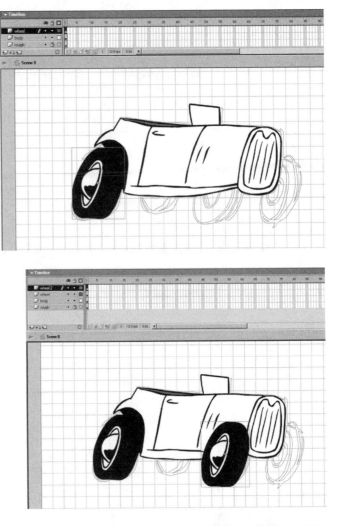

Create a new level on top in the timeline, in the Library select the symbol for the back wheel and drag it onto the stage on our new level.

Resize it and position it as the front wheel.

We now have two wheels but it's just the one symbol. You should look for opportunities to reuse symbols like this wherever you can as it can really help to reduce your file size.

We want to make the wheel move, so we'll need to add some effects. Because we want both wheels to move and we've used the same symbol for both wheels, we need to add these effects to the symbol, not on the stage. So select the symbol in the Library, and then double-click it to enter Edit Symbols mode.

With the timeline for the wheel symbol open. insert a new layer and draw the effect. This is still a static image, so we will need another effect image on another frame to indicate the movement.

Insert a blank keyframe on frame two of the effect level and a keyframe on the wheel level.

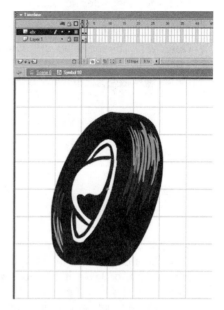

Click the Onion Skin button and draw a new effect slightly different to the previous one on frame 2 of the effect level. We have now turned this symbol into a very simple two-drawing cycle.

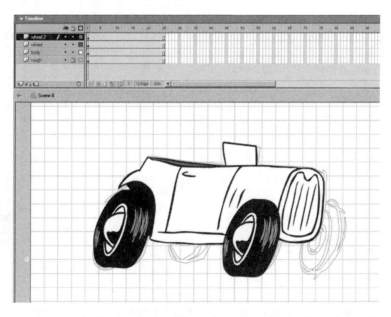

When you return to the scene, both wheels should now have the effects. If you insert frames to the scene, and move along the timeline with the cursor, you should be able to see the cycle moving. Flash is playing the symbol as a looping cycle throughout the scene. We still need the other two wheels though.

Duplicating symbols

We're now going to use duplicating symbols to create our other two wheels. As these wheels are viewed from the other side, we want to get rid of the hubcaps, but by following the next steps we can still use the same symbol.

Open your Library, select the symbol for the wheel, then open the tab at the top right corner and select Duplicate.

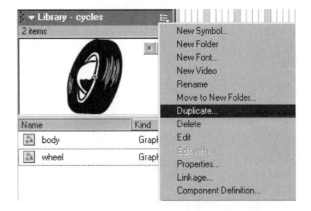

You'll be prompted to name the symbol change if you wish, or leave it named 'wheel copy'. Decide on this and then click OK. You should now have this new symbol in your Library.

Select this symbol and double-click on it to edit the symbol. This gives you the timeline for the new wheel symbol open, we want get rid of the hubcap. So add a new layer and paint a black shape over it.

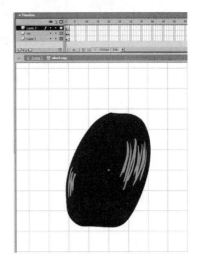

When you return to the scene, add new layers for the new wheels, drag the copied symbol from the Library to the stage, then scale and place them in position. Remember that you'll have to make sure that those layers are below those of the other wheels and of the car body.

Delete your rough layer and you're done. The wheels are all part of the one cycle.

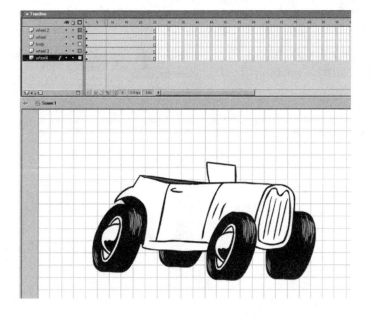

The problem with this scene is that car is moving on the spot, for this animation to work we would need to have the background panning through the shot, to create the illusion of locomotion.

Moving through a scene

Let's say we want the background to be held and the car to drive through scene. What we need to do is convert the entire car – wheels and all – into one symbol.

There are two ways to do this, we can either, copy all the separate layers and then create a new symbol, or we could copy all the separate symbols onto a single layer. We'll copy them all onto a single layer for our new symbol.

Select all the layers and copy them by hitting CTRL/⌘+C, then select Insert > New Symbol.

As our cycle is two frames long, click F6 to insert a new keyframe and then paste the car symbols into this keyframe. You have now created one car symbol.

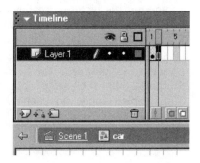

Return to the scene, add a new layer, select the new symbol from the Library and drag it onto the stage.

Delete all the other layers and you should be left with just the new symbol of the car. If you scroll across the timeline, the wheels should spin exactly as they did before. To move the car through the scene, insert a new keyframe and place the two keyframes at opposite ends of the stage. Finally, create motion tweens between the two.

In this case, we have reduced the size of the car to better illustrate what this scene would look like.

The car should now move through the scene with the wheels turning.

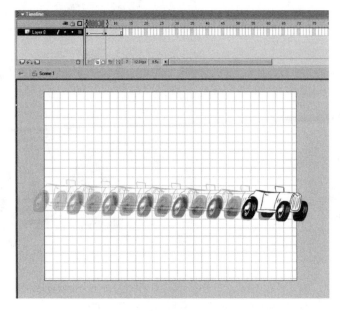

Cycles in perspective

In the last example, we've tweened the cycle of the car through the scene with the two keys the same size. We could also have drawn the same cycle on a different angle, to have the car coming up to camera from the distance. Flash would play and tween the cycle in just the same way.

This is a very basic example of a cycle, but you get the picture. Creating any number of levels and frames as or within a symbol, then placing it on the stage will play the symbol over and over till the end of the scene. In this case there are only two frames to the cycle, but the same principles apply, no matter how many frames the cycle is.

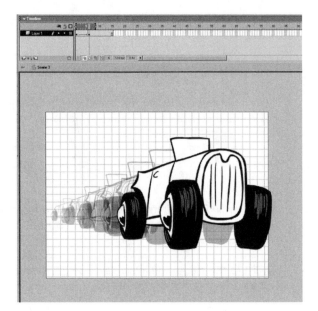

Walk cycles

We discussed the fundamentals of walks and run cycles in the Animation Principles chapter, and also talked, in the Storyboarding chapter, about ways to try to avoid full body walk cycles by creative staging.

Remember also that walks need to contain a lot of different drawings and each of these drawing increases file size, as Flash needs to load and play the new image every frame, and this can cause slower computers to lag.

With all this said, sometimes there is just no way around the fact you have to animate a walk, so let's look at how to do this.

Making a walk cycle in Flash is much the same as the cycle we just made of the car, only more complicated, as there are more drawings and the drawings need to move at a uniform speed. It's best to make these kinds of cycles in the scene, and then copy and paste them as new symbols, like we did with the whole car symbol.

How you animate your walk will depend largely on the way you've designed your character; how fast he needs to walk and his attitude – but the basic one foot in front of the other formula should still apply. There are a few examples of walks and runs in the Animation Principles chapter that you can reference when creating your walks. For this example, we're going to do a double bounce walk.

We've done the first drawing of our walk, and we've broken the character down into four separate elements: legs, body, and two arms. The body, including the head, will move as one, and the arms will swing stridently. So, apart from the legs, all the other elements are one symbol that we can move and tween.

Create a spacing grid to animate the legs to. We've used the grid in Flash to do this, with the grid set at two grid spaces apart for the main keys in the cycle. When all the in-betweens are done, each drawing will move at one grid space.

Next create the different leg drawings following the grid. We've shown them all next to each other in this illustration, but obviously they are all in the one position on the stage over different frames.

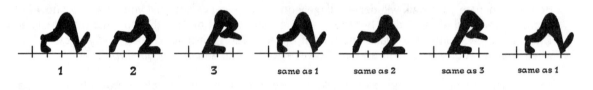

| 1 | 2 | 3 | same as 1 | same as 2 | same as 3 | same as 1 |

Because we've drawn our legs small and in silhouette, we are going to reuse the same three drawings to complete the entire cycle. Convert drawings 1-3 to symbols for re-use, so that the computer will only have to load the images once.

This is the timeline for the scene so far:

Viewed with the Onion Skin function:

Next create the body and arm keys to match the leg positions by inserting keyframes and adjusting the drawings with the Arrow and Rotate tools.

These are all the same symbols, just repositioned. You can add more bounce to your walk by stretching and squashing your drawings at this stage.

Insert blank keyframes for the in-betweens of the legs.

Using the Onion Skin function, create these in-betweens. As we're reusing most of the key drawings for the legs, we only need to make the first three, convert them to symbols, then copy and paste them to the correct frames.

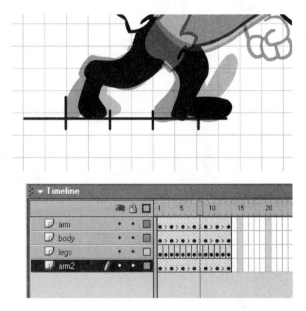

To get the in-betweens for the body and arms use the tweening function, then move the bottom of the arms below the legs, and delete the grid layer.

Here is our entire cycle. By separating levels and reusing as many symbols as possible, we've managed to create a very simple 12 drawing walk cycle with just the nine symbols, a body, two arms and five different legs.

same as 1

> To add a bit more appeal to the walk, you could always animate the tassle on his fez as secondary action, as it's just a line it wouldn't add much to your file size. For our example though, we've kept it held.

You can download this walk cycle from www.friendsofed.com.

Looping

We still need to convert the cycle to a symbol that Flash can play as a loop. All the images on frame 13 are copies of frame one. We needed to put them here to get the tween states for frame 12, the last frame of the cycle. We need to get rid of frame 13 because when it plays as a loop frame one should follow frame 12.

Convert all the tweened images on frame 12 to keyframes by selecting them then hitting F6. Then delete all the frames on frame 13 by selecting them and using SHIFT + F5.

If we now select all the frames of the cycle and copy them, CTRL/⌘ +C, we can create a new symbol and paste them into it, much like we did with our car.

Our walk cycle will be in the Library and we can use it wherever we need.

Panning walk cycles

If we refer back to our original drawing, we see our spacing grid is set at one grid space for each drawing, therefore, if we are using the cycle in place with the background panning, we must ensure that the background pan speed is one grid space per frame to match the feet of the character.

If we are panning the character through a scene, then we must ensure the same spacing applies. The character must move one grid space per frame, 12 grid spaces for each loop of the cycle.

All cycles, whether walk, run, or something more mechanical such as a turning wheel, are invaluable animation tools in Flash. They can save time, keep file size small and are even easier to utilize in Flash than in traditional animation.

Cycles, like most things in animation, should be thoroughly scrutinized to make sure they play smoothly.

> *Test your work often; any small glitches in a cycle can become especially annoying due to the repetition of cycles.*

Animating dialogue in Flash

Animating dialogue in Flash is very similar to animating it in traditional animation. We use the same mouth shapes and follow the same the basic principles of accenting dialogue. In fact, animation in Flash is really just a set of techniques to apply to what you have already learnt about animation, and you use the same ones over and over again.

Understanding how to separate levels, such as mouths and eyes, will make animating dialogue in Flash a very simple task, and being able to save your separate elements as symbols and reuse them will help reduce file size and the amount of work you have to do.

> *For more information on importing sound, including lines of dialogue, please refer back to* Layout 2 – Sound and Testing. *Remember that if you need to sync your sound directly to your animation, then you need to set the sound to* Stream *in the Property inspector.*

We can see in the timeline that we have imported our sound and set it to streaming. We have our mouths on the layer beneath it. By scrolling along the timeline with the cursor, you should be able to hear the sound for each frame, you can then select and expose the mouths that fit the particular sound

The mouth shape you use should fall on, or a frame before, the actual sound. Once you have animated your dialogue, play it back and see how it syncs. Sometimes in Flash, you may need to further advance the mouth shape; maybe two or three frames ahead, depending on the speed of your computer.

Frame 1   *Frame 4*

We will look at animating dialogue much more closely in the film 'The Boy Who Cried Wolf.'

Special effects in Flash

Animation effects seem to be the preoccupation and occasionally, obsession of some Flash animators. A new way to do water or a revolutionary approach to smoke can be the justification for a film. Well, maybe, but you still need a good story and a good script. Effects are an adjunct to the animation process and should be used if not judiciously, then at least appropriately. Your audience will not be held in rapt admiration by the best flame cycle they have ever seen.

Here are some basic Flash effects that can achieve many different results. Like many elements of this program, the potential lies in the imagination of the user.

Alpha settings

The effects we'll cover here will involve the use of alpha settings. We've covered these settings briefly in the Layout chapter when we did our cross-dissolves and fades of the storyboard. So let's look at how to apply these effects to our animation.

Cast shadows

These types of shadows can be used when you have a strong light source like a character near a fire. They are very easy to do in Flash and there are a few ways to do them.

The first way is to create a new layer above the character, and then draw the shadow as a black shape with the Brush tool.

With the shadow selected, convert it to a symbol and adjust the alpha value in the Property inspector. By using the Alpha slide control, you will be able to adjust the shadow to the setting that best suits the scene.

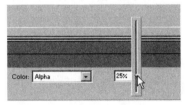

Another way to do this is to simply draw the shadow area on a separate level, as above, using the Brush tool with an alpha setting already picked in the color mixer.

Select black as your fill color, then open the Color Mixer (Window > Color Mixer):

By changing the alpha setting with the slide control here, whatever you draw with the brush will have this alpha setting automatically applied.

You could also create shadows using the Pencil tool, with the tool set to Smooth.

Then draw directly onto the image, using Snap To Object to get the line to meet up perfectly with the edges. You can then use the Color Mixer to fill the shadow area with a color slightly darker than the pre-existing one. Finally, remove the pencil lines and you'll have nice smooth curves without having to redraw. (This method is useful for mouse users where creating a smooth curve is more difficult).

Whichever method you choose, one thing to note is that it's always best to apply these shadows within the symbol of the image. This way, whenever you modify the symbol (say stretch or squash it), the shadow will automatically be modified with it.

Drop shadows

These types of shadows can add a nice look to your animation and are made in exactly the same way as the cast shadow, only on a layer under the character. Whether you create these shadows in the symbol of the image, or as a separate layer in the scene, would depend on what is happening in the scene. Sometimes these shadows move differently to the animation, for example, if the character jumped in the air, the shadow would work separately.

Separate element effects

Sometimes in our animation we require effects like smoke, water, fire etc. Apart from the design and look of these elements, the alpha settings can boost the effect.

This effect is just another example of how we can use the alpha setting in our animation, this smoke could also be done as a cycle.

Learn from everywhere

When animating in Flash, you can take advantage of the principles of traditional, especially limited, animation. These are lessons learned by great artists over many years and are eminently adaptable to the Flash context.

How you adapt these principles and to what level you are prepared to take them, depends on the aims of your film. Obviously, full animation can increase file size dramatically, so if you want to keep the file size small, then you need to limit your animation. Even with these constraints you can create interesting and entertaining films.

> *Remember that anything that moves on the Internet is already more interesting than something that doesn't. Just because you may not have the time to produce studio-quality animation, it doesn't mean that people won't watch it!*

Taking advantage of the Flash program is about working within the program's limitations to produce animated films that transcend those limitations. Always look at your animation and your film as a whole and think about ways that you can use the tools that Flash offers to make the film better.

This is the secret of good Flash films: economy, flexibility and ingenuity. Think small to achieve impressive results.

Over to you

Now it's your turn to take these techniques and apply them to your own animation. Here are some points to remember:

- Start by working rough, this will give your drawings an element of freedom, if you are too concerned with the end product then your drawings risk becoming stilted.

- Stretch and squash your animations, where appropriate to give a feeling of flexibility to your animations, and use pop and cushioning to make the timing more realistic.

- Test, time and refine your animations. Any glitches, in cycles, for example will be magnified in the finished work. It's best to get these things right, right now.

- If you're producing for the Internet, try to keep your key drawings down to a minimum to save file size. Modify your key poses rather than creating fresh in-betweens.

The animation decisions that you make will be determined by the needs of your own film. To help you understand the process a little better in the next chapter we will look at the decisions we made when making 'The Boy Who Cried Wolf'.

9: ANIMATING 'THE BOY WHO CRIED WOLF'

So far we've looked at most of the stages of the filmmaking process from script and storyboard to creating an animatic. We've looked at the principles of animation and how to adapt them when using Flash. Now let's take a look at what you learnt and see how we've applied these lessons to make our short film.

When we left the film at the animatic stage, we had set up all our basic camera moves including our pans, trucks, fades and cross-dissolves. We had roughly timed all these moves and created a foundation on which to build our animation. We'd also imported the sound files for all of our dialogue and placed them in the appropriate scenes. The final step was when we played the animatic in order to check the pacing of our basic film.

So now, let's take a look at how we've taken this animatic and worked it into the finished film. We'll go through each scene in order, and discuss how we've applied some of the lessons we've learned so far to each scene, and expand a little on some of those basic lessons.

All of the FLA files for the movie are available for download from the friends of ED web site. As well as our completed movie, there are FLAs for each scene separately. These are identical in content, but may be easier for you to delve into and investigate. We'll step through the animation decisions and techniques scene-by-scene.

Scene 1

This scene is our establishing shot and where we introduce the audience to the world of the boy who cried wolf and to the boy himself. The main actions in this scene are our camera moves; we've set up all the basic mechanics of these moves already with our storyboard pages in the Layout chapter, but as we talked about in the Storyboarding chapter, we will be creating our backgrounds on several different levels, which will then pan at different speeds to give the scene more depth. So let's start here.

Camera pans

Open up `bcw.sc01.fla` – this is our opening scene in its finished form. We have cleaned up our rough drawings and created separate levels for most of the different elements.

After you've done your finished, clean, drawings don't forget to delete the imported storyboard images – they will take up unnecessary space and slow down the movie.

If you play this FLA now, you should be able to see the different levels moving at different speeds – note the overlay level of the tree, for example.

All the levels pan over the same time, starting on frame 50 and ending on frame 125. Each level contains a pan, which starts on frame 50 and ends on frame 125, as you can see in the timeline.

Start of pan

Stop position of pan

When we first created this pan we had all our elements moving at exactly the same speed; we created the different pan speeds of each element by adjusting the stop position of each level.

The nearest tree, for example, moves a lot further across the stage than the mountains, but in the same number of frames. If you look closely at the start position, you will notice the position of the tree compared to the mountain level. Then if you look at the stop position at frame 125, you can see that the distance between them is no longer the same – the tree has moved much further then the mountains, in other words it's moved faster. The same applies to the sky level, only in reverse – it has moved slower. The ground and village level both pan at the same speed.

By separating the background into these different levels, you can try a variety of different pan speeds to get the effect that works best for the scene.

Cycles

You will notice that when you look at the timeline there are no levels for the sheep and the boy; this is because we have combined them with the ground level, as they will all be panning at the same speed.

To do this, we created the symbols of the sheep and the boy, and then dragged these symbols from the Library into the ground symbol while in Edit Symbols mode, and positioned them accordingly.

This is the timeline for the ground symbol. As you can see, this symbol is not just a held image, it contains several levels of the sheep and is 22 frames long. This is because the sheep symbol is a cycle.

Some animators use movie clips instead of graphic symbols for this purpose. This is easier in a way because you do not need to extend the timeline (a movie clip plays on its own sub-timeline). We find that this method makes timing animations far more complex, as you have to remember exactly how each clip is timed – with graphic symbols, you can see them all at once.

The sheep

This is the timeline for the symbol of the sheep chewing. It has three levels: shadow, body and the head that we have animated to move in a chewing cycle, which is 22 frames long, using just one drawing. We have then placed several instances of the cycle in the timeline of the ground symbol.

For Flash to play the cycle of the sheep inside the ground symbol, it must also contain the same amount of frames as the cycle, and in essence, has become a cycle itself.

It may sound confusing, but what we have is the sheep cycle within the ground symbol, which in itself sits within our main scene. To help you understand this, take a look at the elements of this scene contained within the FLA file for yourself.

You could also achieve this effect by using movie clips, but we have opted to use graphic symbols so that we can check our cycle by scrubbing along the timeline. If we had created our 'chewing' cycle in a movie clip, then Flash would play it in just one frame of the ground symbol.

Sound effects

Another thing to note is that we have imported and placed some sound effects in this scene as well. Sound effects in establishing shots like this really help add atmosphere.

In the Property inspector we have set the bird sound effect to Stream, as we will only use it once and it's a long sound. We have set the lamb sound effect as an Event, because this is a short sound, and will be repeated more than once.

No matter how you've created your sound effects (royalty-free libraries, sitting in a field with a minidisc recorder, or just making the sounds yourself) the principles of placing your sounds are identical.

Scene 2

To examine this scene, open up bcw.sc02.fla. When we created our animatic, we talked about creating a hook-up pose for this scene; a hook up is simply making sure that the position of the last frame of a scene and the position of the first frame of the following scene are the same to help avoid bad continuity and jarring looking cuts.

If you look at the first frame of this scene, you will see that we have used the same symbol of the boy from Scene 1 and enlarged it to match this scene, even though it's only held for two frames, it will help the viewer to follow the cut.

We have made a new background for this scene, to match roughly the same position as the background in Scene 1. It is often possible to resize the same background to reuse, but when cutting to close-ups like this, it's probably best to make a new background with a different horizon line.

If you look at frames three to six, you will notice that we have used stretch and squash techniques to animate the boy. By separating the body and head into separate layers, we can move them independently and give a more natural look to the animation.

Scene 3

The file for this scene is `bcw.sc03.fla`. Once again in this scene we see the use of the classic pop and cushion technique on the villager to the left.

For the other villagers, we have used the simple but effective eye blink as the antic, then made separate mouths, which have been converted to simple two-drawing cycles for the scream.

The character that runs through the scene is a held drawing that has been panned from left to right using motion tweening. For the run back the other way from right to left, we simply flipped him over, by going to Modify > Transform > Flip Horizontal.

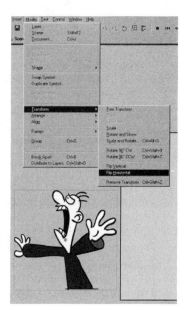

We then enlarged him slightly and placed him on a higher layer so that he appears closer. There are more polished ways to animate this, but since the movement is fast and there is more obvious action happening in the scene, our way will work fine.

Scene 4

In this scene you can see how facial elements can be separated to good effect. Open up `bcw.sc04.fla`, and notice how the eyes and mouths are adjusted to work separately from the rest of the head to create a nice feel to the animation, this also works well when animating dialogue on a character that is moving.

If you look at the mouths on the boy in this scene, you will notice that they move independently from the head and that we have used the motion tweening function to animate this entire scene with only two mouths.

Economical as ever, we have also reused the sky from earlier scenes to save on file size.

At the end of the scene the boy blinks.

The eye blink can be used after a character has finished talking as a nice way to stop him from appearing to suddenly freeze.

Scene 5

In the course of making your film, you should always be on the look out for ways to reuse as many symbols as you can, if you open `bcw.sc05.fla`, you will notice that Scene 5 is very similar to Scene 3, and we have therefore used many of the same elements.

This scene ends with a classic fade to black. We created the fade to black by making a rectangle, which covers the main stage from frames 21 to 35. As you can see in the Property inspector, the rectangle has an Alpha setting of 0 at frame 21, and its opacity gradually rises over the following frames.

Scene 6

We covered the principles of staggers and how to chart them in the Animation Principles chapter . If you look at Scene 6 (`bcw.sc06.fla`), then you'll see that between frames 6 and 17 we have used a stagger to animate the boy's face. This stagger contains all the levels of the boy – his mouth, eyes, head and body.

Staggers

Let's take a quick look at how to do it in Flash.

Create two keyframes, one at frame one and the other at frame five. Place the same symbol in each one. Modify the second image slightly, by stretching it away from the first.

Next create your motion tweens, set Ease to 100 Out.

We now need to create each tween as a keyframe. To do this, select all the tweens and hit F6.

If we were to number these keyframes, 1- 5, then the timing of the scene at the moment would go 1, 2, 3, 4, 5 in order.

Now we need to copy and paste them in the timeline with the stagger timing, which we discussed in the Animation Principles chapter. This timing goes as follows; 1, 2, 3, 2, 3, 4, 3, 4, 5, 4, 5.

So frames 1 to 11, shown here, contain keyframe 1, 2, 3, 2, 3, 4, 3, 4, 5, 4, 5 – in that order.

Scene 7

Scene 7 (bcw.sc07.fla) again reuses many elements from Scene 3 and Scene 5, with the exception of a few new mouths. If we compare the timeline in bcw.sc05.fla, you will see it has been retimed to match the new dialogue for this scene, but all the elements and their positions are the same.

Copying frames to reuse a scene

It may be good practice for you to attempt to do this for yourself. If you would like to, open bcw.sc05.fla again and press CTRL/⌘+ALT +A to select all the frames in Scene 5.

Then hit CTRL/⌘ + ALT + C, go to Scene 7 and with the first frame of the scene selected, paste the frames (CTRL/⌘+ ALT + V).

Scene 7 should now be exactly the same as Scene 5. You now need to retime the characters to match the new dialogue in this scene.

Notice that we have delayed the antic (the blink) of villager two, so that not all the villagers react at once; this creates a better group effect.

Swapping symbols

This is a great technique to use when animating dialogue and you need to make different mouths for characters that you are reusing. You make a duplicate symbol of one of the existing mouths, then edit it.

Add a new layer on top of the existing mouth and draw your new mouth over it in a matching position, then delete the old mouth.

To avoid confusion, rename this new symbol according to the new mouth shape. Then, go back to the scene you need the new mouth in, select the old mouth, and with it highlighted on the stage, right / CTRL-click on it and select Swap Symbol.

A new window will appear with a list of symbols from the Library, you need to select the new mouth shape and Flash will replace the old mouth with the new one.

You sometimes need to create new layers and copy the symbols you wish to swap to that new layer, especially if you're swapping a symbol that has been motion tweened.

This kind of technique can also be used for any number of other symbols such as eyes arms or what ever you need.

Scenes 8, 9, and 10

To examine these scenes, look at bcw.sc08.fla, bcw.sc09.fla, and bcw.sc10.fla. Once again these scenes all reuse symbols from previous scenes. In Scene 8, notice the use of separate elements in this case the head and body are moving independently from each other to create a nice little dialogue touch on the Boy's giggle.

Scene 9 uses elements from the previous scenes, which have been resized and retimed to create an extreme close-up.

Scene 10, again shows the reaction of the villagers, and once more reuses elements from Scenes 5 and 7, but we've re-timed the animation and changed the expression on the eyes.

To achieve this change in expression, we duplicated the existing eyes, changed the expression to one of pure annoyance, and then used the Swap Symbol function to place this into the scene.

In this example, we can see that by changing the expression in a character's eyes, we can completely alter the way the face is read, making it seem like the mouths have been changed when in fact they haven't. This is a way to make an impact whilst saving on file size and animation.

Scene 11

Our final scene, (`bcw.sc11.fla`) is a combination of Scenes 11 and 12 from our original storyboard. For the transition between the two we made a cross-dissolve.

Problems with cross-dissolves

One thing to keep in mind when creating cross-dissolves in Flash, is that whenever you reduce the alpha settings on images that are made up of several symbols together, you will not get a true cross-dissolve (two complete images fading in and out). Flash will dissolve each symbol as a separate image and you will see all the outlines of each symbol through the dissolve.

If you look at the area where the pants meet the shirt, you can clearly see each separate symbol, this kind of thing is an unfortunate problem that Flash has with cross-dissolves. In this case, when you watch the film it won't be so noticeable as we have the image that's fading on top of it as a single symbol. If you think carefully about where and how you use cross-dissolves and fades in Flash, there's no reason to let this kind of problem deter you from doing them – as with everything else, planning and practice will help you solve most problems in animation.

Panning tricks

The other main camera move in this scene is the background pan, unlike Scene 1 where we pan the camera across the background, we pan the background under the camera, so to speak.

It is always a good idea to look at separating your background into separate elements in order to try and minimise the amount of drawing that Flash needs to move, as this can help avoid slow and jerky movements when creating pans.

In this scene we have made the background a gray color card that is held, and we also made a simple cloud shape that moves through the scene to give the impression of the entire background moving.

Trucking tips

Another thing worth noting in this scene is the truck out. If you look at the level of the boy, you can see that because of creating this animation as a cycle, we've only needed use the one instance as it repeats.

By then inserting keyframes at the appropriate points for the truck out and creating motion tweens, Flash will automatically play each frame of the cycle over the truck out. This is a very useful function and you'll find you use it a lot the more you get used to it.

We've done this truck out following on from our animatic, in its most basic form. Another way to do this truck out would be to combine all of the layers into one symbol and then create the truck out using that symbol on one layer.

Doing things this way can save a lot of time, but care must be taken to make sure all the animation within the symbol works and is the correct length for the scene.

The first screening

Now you've investigated each scene in our film individually, open the whole movie up in Flash (that's the `boy who cried wolf.fla`) and test it. I think you'll agree it has turned out rather well.

We've tried to make this film as simple as possible and have included within it most of the basic camera moves, and what we consider useful animation techniques and tips.

As we've said many times throughout this book, there are no right or wrong ways to do things, but there are principles that need to be understood in order to find the most effective ways to do things.

Because we provided you with the Flash files for this film, if there's anything we didn't cover in the text of this chapter, you will be able to work it out for yourself by examining these files on your own. A good way of learning is to investigate how others have done it. If you come across any particular problems then you can always get in touch with us via `support@friendsofED.com`, and we'll be glad to hear from you.

But of course, we're not quite finished. We made the film, we're happy, but what's the point if no one else can see it? Unless you're thinking of inviting each member of your audience around to your home, and knowing some of them, we don't advise it, you need to get your movie out there. That's what we'll look at in the next chapter, publishing and outputting your masterwork.

Over to you

Hopefully you'll have completed your Flash film by this stage, but if you've been having difficulties, take this opportunity to compare your process with ours, and see if you can pick up any tips. You could learn in a sentence something that has taken other Flash animators weeks and months of toil to discover, by which we mean ourselves of course! To recap you should have:

- A finalized FLA file containing your move, that plays without glitches and has all of the camera movements, animation and sound that you'd envisaged.

You're now ready to start thinking seriously about outputting your film, whether to the Internet or onto video tape – and that's what we'll look at in the next chapter.

10: OUTPUT & PUBLISHING

So now that you've finished your movie, it's time to find fame and fortune by outputting and publishing, whether over the Internet or via video. In this chapter we will look at some of the options available to you now, and consider the best way to show your masterpiece to your adoring public.

The first thing to consider is whether your movie is destined to be shown over the Internet, or whether you are going to use a video-editing package to publish the film as a video. The first option is the one that most people use when starting out in Flash animation. It is a very cheap and easy way to reach the outside world and, who knows, before long you could have gained yourself a cult following.

By default, Flash will output your movie as a SWF file, which stands for Shockwave for Flash. SWF files can be played by the Flash player – if you are aiming your film at a web savvy audience, and you are assuming that they are regular web surfers, then it's a fair guess that most of your audience will have a Flash 5 player installed.

You are not limited to outputting your movie as a SWF file, you can also output your movie in a variety of other file types, these include: QuickTime MOV, AVI, or as a sequence of images like JPEGs or BMPs, to name but a few. If you want to publish your movie for video or something other then a standard SWF file for the Internet, you will probably need to consider one of these options. The choice you make here will depend largely on the type of software you intend to use to do your editing or make the transfer to tape. We will look at ways to output your movie to video later in the chapter.

Preparing for the Internet

Before we rush off and whack our movie up on the net for all to see, there are a few last important steps to take. When people view your film over the Internet, the film will automatically start to play. Unfortunately, unlike looking at the SWF on your computer when you test your movie, the audience does not have the entire movie saved on their hard drive and can only watch as much of it as their computer can download. Therefore, if they have a slow Internet connection, the movie will keep pausing while they wait for frames to download onto their computer.

This problem is resolved by making a loading scene for the movie. This scene will either play until enough of the film has been downloaded for the film to play without freezing, or it can be set to wait until the film has downloaded 100% to ensure smooth viewing. The choice is ultimately yours, but we would advise the latter, however the techniques used to create the preloader are the same, so let's look at this process now.

Preloaders

The loading scene, or **preloader**, will prevent the film from starting until enough of the movie has been downloaded for the viewers computer to play the entire film without it freezing.

But how do we know how much of the film needs to download before it can be played? Well, to check this we need to look at the Bandwidth Profiler. This will show us how the movie streams, in other words how fast the movie is downloaded and whether it will stop in places to wait for certain frames to be downloaded.

If you've got your movie open as we go through this, you'll find it easier to understand. If you want to see the exact same figures as we have, open the boy who cried wolf.fla (downloaded from www.friendsofED.com).

To view the Bandwidth Profiler, first test your movie by clicking CTRL/⌘ + ENTER. Then select View> Bandwidth Profiler.

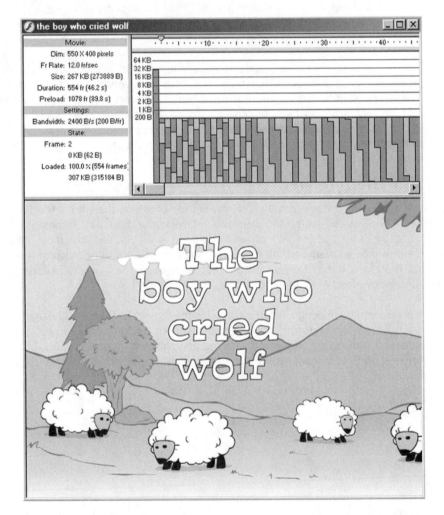

You will then see a type of graph above your movie. This shows each frame of the movie and how much data has to be downloaded on that frame before it can be played. The Profiler also shows the duration of the movie in seconds, the number of frames, and total file size.

The red line at the bottom of the graph shows the file size per frame that can be downloaded for the movie to play without stopping. In this case we set it assuming the download speed is a 28.8k modem and it's 200B.

You can adjust your settings here. By selecting Debug > 56k (4.5 KB/s), you cater for 56k, and likewise for other download speeds. We prefer to set it to 28.8k so that the movie can be watched by all but those with the very slowest connections.

If you look along the Bandwidth Profiler you will notice that the file size is quite high at frame one, ranging from 16 to 32 kb. The large file size is due to the fact that all the symbols used for the entire first scene, including the event sounds, are loaded here. The file size drops dramatically afterwards, as Flash is simply reusing all the same symbols for the rest of the scene so there is no need to load any more images until the next scene. Of course, at the beginning of the next scene we will see a sharp rise in file size again.

By selecting any frame in the Bandwidth Profiler, Flash will take you to that frame so you can see where your streaming problems are.

To test how your film will stream over the Internet, you simply select View > Show Streaming.

You will notice now that Flash will play the movie exactly as it would appear to someone over the net. Notice how it stops and starts as it waits for frames to download. This is exactly what we will fix with the loading scene.

Making a preloader

You've probably seen a million different loading scenes – some are inspirational, some are funny and others are just crazy. No matter what they look like, in essence they all do pretty much the same thing. For now, we'll make a very simple one. Our aim is to make a font that blinks on for 3 frames and off for 3 frames until the movie is loaded.

The safest way to make a preloader is to ensure that all of the movie is loaded onto the user's computer. Let's look at how to do this now.

1. To make our loading scene we will make a new scene and place it ahead of Scene 1. To do this, go to Scene 1 then Insert > New Scene and call it 'loading'.

2.   To move this scene ahead of Scene 1, select Window > Scene to bring up the Scene Selector window. Then simply grab the new loading scene and move it above Scene 1, this will place it at the beginning of the movie.

3.   Within the loading scene insert a keyframe on frame one, and another on frame six. On frame one select a typeface of your choice and type 'loading' in the middle of the stage.

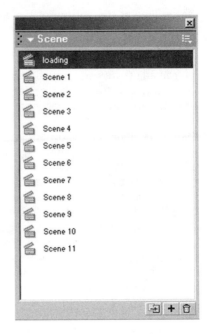

4.   The font we've used is called 'Mirisch', we use it a lot as you may see at www.funnyazhell.com. If you use a non- standard font like this, it may impact a little on file size. If this going to be crucial it's best to use the three at the top of the drop-down box. Each is named with an underscore (_) first.

5.   Next insert a blank keyframe on frame four.

6.   Add another layer, which will be for our actions, telling the scene what to do. Rename this new layer 'action' and our other layer 'font'.

7.   Now insert a keyframe at frame six on the action layer.

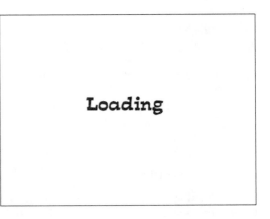

The first thing we want the scene to do is to keep repeating – playing over and over until the movie is loaded. To do this we will need to put a movie control action into our film.

8. Select frame six in the action layer, then hit F9 or go to Window > Actions to open the Actions panel at the bottom of the screen. Select Actions > Movie Control and then double-click goto.

9. Change the settings to match those in this screenshot:

Here we are adding a piece of ActionScript gotoAndPlay(1); on frame six. Telling Flash that on frame six of the current scene, our loading scene, it should go back to frame one and start playing.

> *This action means that each time the scene reaches frame six it will go back to the first frame and play the scene over again in a never-ending loop.*

10. Now, go back to the timeline and select frame one. You should notice a small *a* in the box for frame six, this means that an action has been added to this frame.

11. Go back to the Actions panel and select Actions > Conditions/Loops and double-click on if.

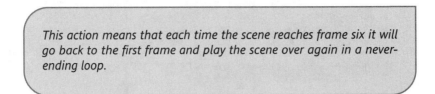

You need to add a conditional to the box, which will determine if enough of our movie has loaded.

Exactly how high you set this figure is up to you. If you set it to the exact number of frames that your movie has (in this case 534), then you will get optimal performance on everyone's computer, but the loading times will be longer. Our technique is to find the right balance.

> *If your target audience are likely to have older computers, then the total frame count is a safer figure here – it also removes all the guesswork and testing we're about to do.*

The 'balanced' figure will vary depending on your movie and how well it streams, you will usually have to test it a few times to get it right. Start with a number somewhere in the middle of your total frame count for the movie.

If your movie is 1000 frames long, set it at 500. This is what we're going to do here.

The conditional we need is:

`Number of fames loaded Greater Than Preload frame number`

Luckily Flash gives us a term we can use for the number of frames loaded, which it calculates itself (this is `_framesLoaded`).

12. Type in the conditional '`_framesLoaded > 500`' (or your own choice of number).

We now need to tell Flash *what* to do when frame 500 is loaded. In this case, we want it to play the movie starting from frame one, Scene 1.

13. So select Actions > Movie Control and click goto.

14. Change the Scene: drop-down to read Scene 1.

15. Ensure that Go to and Play is selected.

The ActionScript in the panel will now read:

```
if (_framesLoaded > 500) {
    gotoAndPlay("Scene 1", 1);
}
```

If you've played safe and used the total frame route, you've finished your preloader. The rest of us have some testing to do.

Fine-tuning your preloader

As mentioned before the amount of frames we've told our preloader to load is just an approximation.

To check and adjust this, we need to test the movie, and select View > Show Streaming again.

What should happen next is that Flash will start to play the loading scene over and over; you can see the small arrow at the top of the timeline moving back and forth through the scene. If you look at the top of the Bandwidth Profiler, you will notice that there is a green bar at the top of the frame that is moving along the timeline, this is showing you how much of the movie is loaded.

If you scroll along with it when it gets to frame 500, it will start to play the movie. The arrow on the timeline will now also start to move along at the rate the film is playing. By watching the green bar and the arrow you can see the distance between how much of the film is loaded and where the film is up to. If there is not enough of the film loaded, the arrow will catch up to the green bar and the film will stop. If you have loaded more of the film than you need, the green bar will reach the end of the film before the film itself ends.

You can adjust the amount of frames loaded by selecting frame one of the loading scene where the action is, and changing the figure in the conditional.

As it turned out for our film, 500 was a pretty good approximation. You can check out this version of the FLA if you download it from the friends of ED web site (it's called boy_preloader.fla).

Stop buttons and looping

If you leave your movie as it is, it will load, play and then loop around forever. This is fine, but you may want to add a button onto the end of your film asking the viewer if they would like to watch again.

Usually you would place a stop action on the last frame of your movie to stop it from going back and playing the movie over again, and add a play again button.

Adding a play again button

On the very last frame of the last scene of your movie, you need to add the piece of scripting that stops the movie from looping.

1. Open your FLA up into Flash and navigate to the last scene (in our case Scene 11). Scroll along to the end of the timeline.

2. Add another layer, and call it 'action'. To keep the timeline ordered, you may want to drag this right to the top.

3. Select the last frame and make it a blank keyframe. Open up the Actions panel (F9).

4. Select Actions> Movie Control and double-click on stop.

    This adds the ActionScript stop(); to the frame. This will stop the movie in its tracks. What we need to do now is to add a button asking the question "Play Again?".

    The button we're going to add will be very basic, as with a lot of this part of the chapter, you can delve much deeper into the workings of Flash if you wish.

5. Add yet another layer on top of your timeline, and rename it 'button'.

6. Select the last frame in it a make it a blank keyframe.

7. Using the Text tool, write a nice message.

8. With the Arrow tool, select your text box and convert it into a symbol (Insert > Convert to Symbol... or F8).

9. Call it 'again', and instead of a graphic symbol, make it a Button.

10. Double-click on the button, to get into Edit Symbols mode.

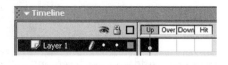

You will notice that a button symbol has a different type of timeline to others – it's a little too indepth to explain the reasons why here. If you are interested in more than we cover here, then there are a wealth of Flash instructional books on the market, Flash MX Express for example (ISBN: 1903450950), will tell you all you need to know.

11. Insert a keyframe in the frame labeled Hit.

> *The content of the Hit frame determines the area of the screen which the button occupies. This can be more or less than the graphical content. The content of the Hit frame is not seen.*

With text, it is best to make the 'hit' area a rectangle that covers all of the writing. So that's what we'll do.

12. Draw a filled rectangle that covers all of the text on the Hit frame.

13. Return to the main scene now by clicking on Scene 11. With the button still selected, open the Actions panel.

14. Select Actions > Movie Control and double-click on goto.

15. We want the button to send the viewer back to the start of Scene 1, so the options should be selected thus:

16. That's it! Test your move and you'll see something akin to this after all the action:

The FLA with the button included is `boy_play again.fla` in the downloadable code files.

Whatever options you've gone for all that is left now is the final SWF creation and publishing your movie.

Publishing your movie for the Internet

Flash makes publishing your movie for the Internet simple by enabling you to publish it as an SWF and a HTML file with the SWF embedded within it. This means that you can upload your HTML page and SWF directly to your web site without having to do any fancy HTML coding or needing some sort of web page building program. Before you publish your movie, there are some settings that need to be addressed.

By default, Flash will publish the movie as an SWF file and an HTML file with the SWF embedded into it, which is just what we want in this instance.

Select File > Publish Settings, and click on the Flash tab.

The settings we will be concerned with here are:

Version: This will determine which version of the Flash player you will need to play the movie.

Flash Player 6 is the latest version at the time of writing and will produce the most compressed (smallest) SWF. At the time of writing, an awful lot of people still only have Flash 5 player, but luckily there is nothing in our FLA that won't work in version five, or version four for that matter.

> *To enable the widest audience possible for your movie, select Flash Player 4.*

Load order: This will determine which way Flash loads the layers in your film, since we've made a loading scene, this really wont effect our movie, so use the default setting.

Protect from import: This option does exactly what it says. Stops people from being able to take you swf file and import it back into Flash and steal all your hard earned secrets!

Audio Stream / Audio Event: These settings will determine the quality that Flash publishes your sound files at. If you have not set them individually in the movie, you can adjust the movie as a whole here.

By default, Flash will publish your sounds at 16kbps. Increasing the bit rate will improve the quality of the sound, but will also increase the file size. By trying a few different settings and checking the file size against the quality of the sound, you can best decide which is more important.

All these settings will affect the way Flash publishes your SWF file.

Flash also publishes the movie as a HTML file with the SWF embedded. This basically means that it can be viewed as a web page in your browser. Select the HTML tab to view these settings.

These settings will affect the way Flash publishes your HTML page. At this stage the default settings will do fine, as most of these settings relate to web site stuff, which is a whole different can of worms.

Now that we've told Flash how we want it to publish our movie, simply hit Publish.

Flash will now have placed an SWF file and a HTML file in the directory where you have the main FLA file. They will both be labeled the same as the FLA file.

boy_play again.fla boy_play again.html boy_play again.swf

If you double-click on the HTML file icon, it should open your browser and play the file as it would be seen by someone viewing it on the web. You can now edit the HTML file if you wish, for example, changing its background color to match your movie, or the rest of your web site.

Once you're happy with the movie and the way it's been published, you can then upload your web site, using whatever methods and programs you choose.

Video output

If you decide to output your film to video, you are going to need some other software. Flash itself does not connect to video devices – to control them you will need a video editing package. If you have a newer computer, you may already have one installed, Macs have iMovie, and Windows XP users have Movie Maker. You'll also need connecting leads and maybe extra computer hardware if you don't have the correct port installed in your machine.

Whichever you choose, and there are many at many different price points, you have to export your from Flash in a format that will allow your program to import it.

Whatever program or file format you are using, there are two things that you need to be aware of:

Interactivity: It may sound a obvious point, but on video there can be no interactivity. We have to output a Flash movie without buttons or ActionScripting of any kind. We don't need a preloader either.

Compression: It is always better to export your movie from Flash uncompressed in any way.

> *A good general rule, with all file transfer between computers, is that you should always perform the compression at the last possible stage. If you compress the movie as it is exported from Flash it will not be of as high a quality when it finally gets to video tape.*

Be aware of just how large uncompressed video files are – you'll need a lot of hard drive space.

There are slight differences between the exporting procedure on a PC and that on a Mac, so we'll quickly run through each separately. Video exporting is a notoriously complex subject, so if you intend to do this often, we'd recommend that you take advice. There are many books on different video software (iMovie, Premiere, Final Cut Pro and After Effects all have friends of ED books devoted to them) that will cover the subject in far greater depth than we could possibly do here. For further tips you could try Internet message boards and newsgroups – www.friendsofED.com/forums is one place you could start.

Exporting a movie on a PC

The standard video file format for PCs is the AVI file. So that's what we'll cover here.

1. You should have your movie open in Flash. Open the boy who cried wolf.fla if you haven't one to practice on.

2. Select File > Export Movie and you'll see a traditional file browser appear, the Export Movie window. In the Save as type: drop-down, select Windows AVI (*.avi).

3. Browse to your preferred directory and type your File name: in the box. Click Save.

    A dialog box giving options for exporting as an AVI file will open:

You would think that leaving the Compress video box unchecked would create an uncompressed file, and it will, but it is best to have more control of the options. In order to get to these options, we have to check the box.

4.   Check the Compress Video box, select the best Sound Format: option – that's 44kHz 16 Bit Stereo, roughly CD quality.

5.   Leave the other options as they are and click OK.

6.   Select Compressor to be Full Frames (Uncompressed) and click OK.

Wait a while and your file will be exported ready for manipulation in your preferred video editor.

Exporting a movie on a Mac

The standard video file format for Macs is the MOV, QuickTime file, so that's what we'll cover here.

1. Open your movie in Flash – as always we're using the boy who cried wolf.fla.

2. Select File > Export Movie.

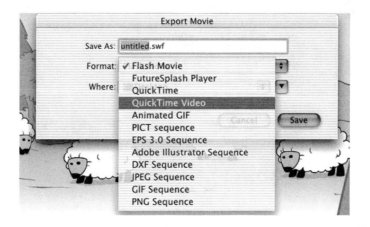

3. The Export Movie dialog box has a Format: option. The particular type of QuickTime file we want to select from the drop-down is QuickTime Video.

4. Type the file name for your MOV file in the Save As: box, and use the Where: drop-down to select exactly where you wish the file to be exported to. Click Save.

    A dialog box containing the options for exporting in the QuickTime Video format will open:

5.   Set the options as shown in this screen shot:

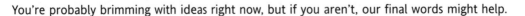

6.   Click OK and your file will be exported. After it has been saved, you will be able to open it in your video editor

That's all folks

We've finished our movie, and it's ready to show to people. Get ready for the feature film offers to come rolling on in.

Over to you

Having made your animated masterpiece, you've got to think about your target audience and how best to get your film to them. You need to consider:

- If you're going to distribute it over the Internet, you need to think about modem and CPU speeds and build a preloader accordingly.

- Do you want to include a 'play again' button or any other sort of interactivity, or make alterations to the HTML page that Flash will export.

- What video editing program you may use if you want to output your film to tape.

There are a myriad of options to consider in getting your movie out to the public and the movie moguls. These decisions may seem to be a little of an afterthought, but they are really important – you want everyone to see your film in its best light.

You're probably brimming with ideas right now, but if you aren't, our final words might help.

OVER TO YOU

Filmmaking, whether it's live action, animation, 2D or 3D offers a great forum for self expression. Flash allows the individual, the little guy, to have a voice and the Internet presents a unique opportunity to distribute their films.

This book has given you the skills to confidently tackle any kind of animated film you want to make. Just remember, as we've said many times in this book, a film is something you build. Even the most avant-garde approach requires discipline and knowledge of the filmmaking process - you have to know the rules before you can break them.

The making of any film starts with an idea. Where that idea comes from is up to you. You can come up with something totally original or adapt one from some other source. There are very few completely original ideas, instead people find inspiration elsewhere. The difference between being influenced by and ripping off someone else's work is probably a matter of degree and also what you bring to that concept or idea to make it your own and say what you have to say with your own voice.

If you seek to be inspired, make sure you're inspired by the right people. Look at the filmmakers you admire and figure out what it is that makes their films successful (and we're not necessarily talking box office here). Study their shots and camera moves, how they frame scenes and pace the action. Copy some of their shots if you think you can use them. Look at the work of the great directors; Hitchcock, John Ford, Fellini, Scorsese, Chuck Jones! There are many great filmmakers and no end of inspiration.

What we've outlined in this book are the stages you need to take your film through to produce a cohesive and hopefully entertaining statement. A film is something you build! If you're not happy with your project at any stage, don't proceed to the next until you are. Take a story or idea that you find interesting and translate that to a script and storyboard that works. If it doesn't entertain you, then chances are it won't entertain anyone else.

Be critical of your work and don't be too ready to pat yourself on the back. Set high standards for yourself. An audience doesn't differentiate between a one minute Flash film and a seventy minute feature extravaganza. If they watch a film they want to be entertained by it. They don't have a switch in their heads that lowers their expectations according to the cost of the film they're looking at. A good film is a good film whether it's animated, 2D, 3D, live action or Flash. A cartoon should never be considered any less an artistic statement.

Flash offers opportunities for the individual filmmaker that have never before existed. Take advantage of this opportunity and make the most of it. Don't be intimidated, take chances, but try to hone your skills and improve your knowledge. Watch films and read books.

Here are some books about animation and filmmaking we recommend you consider:

- The Illusion of Life: Disney Animation by Frank Thomas and Ollie Johnston. (ISBN: 0786860707)
- Cartoon Animation by Preston Blair. (ISBN: 0929261518)
- The Five C's Of Cinematography by Joseph V. Mascelli. (ISBN: 187950541X)
- In The Blink Of An Eye by Walter Murch. (ISBN: 1879505622)

And here's our final tip:

In filmmaking, especially in Hollywood, it seems the hardest part about writing a film is coming up with an ending. Projects are pitched, scripts are written and films are even put into production without any idea of how to resolve them, so if you start a film, make sure you've got an ending. If, like many filmmakers before you, you've written yourself into a corner, you can always fall back on the old chestnut (we haven't seen it used for a while):
"... and then I woke up!"

Index

The index is arranged hierarchically, in alphabetical order, with symbols preceding the letter A. Many second-level entries also occur as first-level entries. This is to ensure that you will find the information you require however you choose to search for it.

friends of ED particularly welcomes feedback on the layout and structure of this index. If you have any comments or criticisms, please contact: feedback@friendsofED.com

friendsofed.com/forums

J oin the friends of ED forums to find out more about our books, discover useful technology tips and tricks, or get a helping hand on a challenging project. *Designer to Designer*™ is what it's all about—our community sharing ideas and inspiring each other. In the friends of ED forums, you'll find a wide range of topics to discuss, so look around, find a forum, and dive right in!

■ **Books and Information**

Chat about friends of ED books, gossip about the community, or even tell us some bad jokes!

■ **Flash**

Discuss design issues, ActionScript, dynamic content, and video and sound.

■ **Web Design**

From front-end frustrations to back-end blight, share your problems and your knowledge here.

■ **Site Check**

Show off your work or get new ideas.

■ **Digital Imagery**

Create eye candy with Photoshop, Fireworks, Illustrator, and FreeHand.

■ **ArchivED**

Browse through an archive of old questions and answers.

HOW TO PARTICIPATE

Go to the friends of ED forums at **www.friendsofed.com/forums**.

Visit **www.friendsofed.com** to get the latest on our books, find out what's going on in the community, and discover some of the slickest sites online today!

Notes

Notes

Notes

Notes

Notes